MW00436206

Tales of Risotto
Culinary Adventures from Villa d'Este

Tales of RISOTTO

Culinary Adventures
from Villa d'Este

Jean Govoni Salvadore and Luciano Parolari

Preface by Mitchell Davis, James Beard House

Glitterati
INCORPORATED

New York, New York

First published 2006 by

Glitterati Incorporated
225 Central Park West
New York, New York 10024
www.GlitteratiIncorporated.com

First edition, 2006

Design by Sarah Morgan Karp
Library of Congress Cataloging-in-Publication data

200 692 5135

Hardcover ISBN 0-9777531-3-1

Printed and bound in China by Hong Kong Scanner Arts, Inc.

10 9 8 7 6 5 4 3 2 1

This book is dedicated to Jean-Marc Droulers, in gratitude for his unfaltering support, and to the staff of the Hotel, all of whom assisted in the compilation of this book and its recipes.

Table of Contents

Recipes

Cheese Risottos

Vegetable And
Fruit Risottos

Fish Risottos

Black Squid Ink Risotto   70
Risotto Nero alle Seppie

Risotto with Perch Fillets   72
Risotto con Pesce Persico

Risotto with Seafood   74
Risotto ai Frutti di Mare

Risotto with Stuffed Cuttlefish and Basil   76
Risotto con Seppioline Farcite e Basilico

Risotto with Smoked Salmon   78
Risotto al Salmone Affumicato

SHELLFISH RISOTTOS

Risotto with Lemon and Shrimp   80
Risotto al Limone con Scampi

Risotto with Lobster and Crayfish   82
Risotto con Aragosta e Gamberi

Risotto Mantecato with Clams, Zucchini   85
Blossoms, and Wild Asparagus
Risotto Mantecato con Vongole Veraci,
Fior di Zucchine, e Asparagi Selvatici

Risotto with Prosecco Sparkling   86
Wine and Oysters
Risotto con Prosecco e Ostriche

Risotto with Scallops Flavored with Rosemary   88
Risotto con Noci di Capesante al Rosmarino

Risotto and Shrimp Carthusian   90
Risotto alla Certosina

SEASONAL RISOTTOS

AUTUMN

Risotto with Pumpkin Blossoms
and White Truffles
Risotto con Fiori di Zucca e Tartufo Bianco

94

WINTER

Milanese Risotto with Saffron
Risotto alla Milanese

98

Ossobuco Milanese
Ossobuco alla Milanese

101

SPRING

Risotto with Spring Vegetables
Risotto Primavera

104

SUMMER

Risotto with Green Tomatoes,
Crispy Bacon, and Fava Beans
*Risotto con i Pomodori Verdi, la Pancetta
Affumicata Croccante, e le Fave*

109

Poultry And Meat Risottos

Risotto with Chicken
Risotto con il Pollo

112

Risotto with Chicken Leftovers
Risotto con Avanzi di Pollo

114

Risotto with Chicken Livers
Risotto con Fegatini di Pollo

115

Two Great Houses

It seems only fitting that two great houses known for fine food should converge on a gastronomic project such as this book. While the Beard House was established in 1986, the year 2003 marked James Beard's centennial. During his lifetime, Villa d'Este welcomed Beard several times to its idyllic setting on the shores of Lake Como. And the Beard House is happy to have been able to welcome the Villa's chef, Luciano Parolari, not once, but twice, to cook in James Beard's kitchen in New York.

When culinary icon James Beard bought the townhouse at 167 West 12th Street in Manhattan's Greenwich Village neighborhood in 1973, he certainly had no idea it would become a mecca for the country's top chefs, nor that such an organization would ever carry his name. Originally built in 1840, the house had only had three owners before Beard took the deed. During his life, it was more than just a home—it was a cooking school, a party space, and, most important, a meeting place for America's culinary talent. Among those who would drop in to break bread with Jim were Julia Child, Jacques Pépin, Madhur Jaffrey, Paula Wolfert, Rose Levy Beranbaum, and virtually every other familiar name on the American food scene today.

Through the trees, Lake Como looks as though it was arranged by an artist.

After Beard died in 1985, his friends decided that something should be done with his house to maintain its place as a culinary crossroad. On the advice of Julia Child, Peter Kump—then owner of a cooking school—raised enough money for a down payment on the property. Several people contributed time and money to help get the foundation going. Barbara Kafka and Wolfgang Puck were among the first to host fundraising events at the house. It didn't take long to realize that these sorts of events—special gastronomic dinners prepared by renowned chefs and paired with fine wines—were appealing to a broad audience. Soon the format for the Beard House events was born.

Today the James Beard Foundation invites more than three hundred chefs annually to perform on the culinary stage that is provided by the James Beard House. Nightly dinners, Friday lunches, Saturday workshops, and all sorts of events in-between provide the meat for our mission of promoting American gastronomy. Other important Foundation endeavors include a culinary scholarship program that distributes annually more than $400,000 to help students pay for the high cost of culinary education. The annual James Beard Foundation Awards give credit where credit is due in the fields of restaurants, chefs, wine, food journalism, books, food-related broadcasting, restaurant design, and other related categories. In addition, the Foundation archives and library are invaluable resources for culinary research. A series of publications keeps members informed about the goings-on in the food world, not just in America but around the world as well.

Like a fine *Risotto alla Milanese* paired with a heady glass of Barolo, the pairing of Villa d'Este and the James Beard House is a delicious match.

Mitchell Davis
James Beard House
New York City

Risotto: Mainstay of Northern Italy

Until thirty or forty years ago, Italian cooking was synonymous with spaghetti and meatballs. This is no longer the case. Italian cuisine and its regional varieties are so popular today that there are thousands of books and websites dedicated to its exploration. *Tales of Risotto* concentrates on the food central to northern Italy through the eyes and ears of Luciano Parolari. As Executive Chef at the Villa d'Este, Parolari is known through culinary circles to be one of the premier experts on risotto.

Until the early 1970s, little was understood internationally about the importance of rice to Italian cooking. The advent of international air travel from the Americas and Australia assisted in this discovery. Visitors to the region came to understand that Italian home cooking—especially in the north—is quite different from what was considered Italian food in their home countries.

Extra virgin olive oil, Parmigiano-Reggiano, saffron, porcini mushrooms, white truffles (only available in the province of Alba in Piedmont), Florentine T-bone steak, the most tender veal, prosciutto crudo, red radicchio salad from Treviso, asparagus, and artichokes are only a few of the items that are considered basic ingredients for refined Italian palates. The truth is that Italians can be quite extravagant in preparing their meals, as it is just one of the art forms we take so seriously. Italian cooking is based on quality ingredients, which is why it is considered to be one of the most expensive cuisines in the gastronomic world. The most sought-after dish is risotto— and it has become very trendy because it is both delicious and healthly.

That brings me to the question, why this book about risotto? For the answer, we have to go back a few years.

In 1973, the Villa d'Este Hotel celebrated its one-hundredth year as a hotel. And to mark this anniversary, a cooking school was inaugurated at the hotel and run by Luciano Parolari, who was then the chef of The Grill and became Executive Chef for the hotel in 1978. As Villa d'Este was among the very first hotels to create a cooking school, it became quite the rage. Word spread and groups of food lovers, mostly from the United States, crowded the Villa d'Este kitchens.

In 1975, Julie Dannenbaum, who was running the cooking school of the Gritti Palace Hotel in Venice, dropped by to meet Luciano and asked him to be a guest at her Creative Cooking School in Philadelphia. Thanks to Julie, Villa d'Este was repeatedly invited to give demonstrations for various benefit events, and consequently our recipes were in great demand in the United States. At that time, we initiated a tradition of sending out Christmas cards with a full menu made up from our kitchen's delights, which we continue to this day, and our audience and following has grown as each message is delivered.

Then in 1978 Chuck Williams, the founder of Williams-Sonoma, invited Luciano to San Francisco to prepare a gala dinner for a fundraiser with an Italian theme. Before the dinner, Luciano gave a cooking demonstration of the menu about to be served. A few days later at the Beverly Wilshire Hotel, Luciano gave another demonstration, followed by a tasting for another charity event. The demonstrations were a hit with high society. The Beverly Wilshire event drew over three hundred people, and Luciano made a risotto. This was the first time that risotto had been introduced to so large a crowd, and certainly a first for the West Coast.

That same winter, friends of the hotel from Augusta, Georgia—Sissie and Billy Morris—asked if Luciano would be available to give a cooking demonstration to raise funds for the Augusta Symphony Orchestra. We were delighted to accept the invitation, and this is how we started the ball rolling on international cooking demonstrations. Requests for Luciano started pouring in, and thus Villa d'Este went on to launch the first cooking school tour in the United States, introducing fine northern Italian cuisine, and featuring our trademark risottos.

Since that time Luciano has gone on to gain a worldwide reputation as one of Italy's major chefs and has been called the "King of Risotto". So we have here a book that not only focuses on northern Italian home cooking, but one that offers the recipes of one of the region's most famous chefs.

One story clearly sums up the dining experience that Luciano Parolari has created at Villa d'Este, which, of course, is not just about food, but about the total experience:

A journalist arrived incognito and decided to sample the food at The Grill Restaurant. It was a lovely summer evening and dinner was served under the hotel's landmark plane trees in the gardens overlooking Lake Como. The journalist told Salvatore Piazza, the maitre d', that she would like to order the speciality of the region, risotto, but that according to the menu the order was for a minimum of two people. Mr. Piazza was heard to say, "Not to worry. You order one, I'll order one!"

How did we discover this episode? The journalist, a syndicated columnist, wrote an article that was promptly forwarded to us!

Luciano Parolari and his world-famous risotto still travel the world today, most recently at a gala dinner at the James Beard Foundation in New York celebrating his Silver Jubilee (twenty-five years) as Executive Chef of the hotel. It was after 10 p.m. when Luciano made his appearance to take his bows and to receive the applause of the guests who crowded the rooms.

The five-course meal was a great success, with Risotto with Pumpkin Blossoms and Alba Truffles the most mouthwatering and distinctive dish on the menu. Everybody was asking for the recipe and Luciano—in all modesty—said that it was the white truffle that had been smuggled through New York Immigration that made all the difference. Not true—even the plainest risotto cooked by Luciano is a work of art.

At this point, Luciano had to explain how he was able to bring in the truffle. I was accompanying Luciano at the time, acting as his spokesperson and interpreter. We were on our way out of Customs, but we couldn't shake off a dog that kept sniffing our bags. I was sure the dog recognized in me the dog lover that I am, but Luciano squelched my enthusiasm by saying, "The dog is after my truffle!"

Sure enough, we were asked to step aside and Luciano's carry-on bag was turned inside out. I ran my pitch about how I had consulted the American consulate before leaving Italy and I had been assured that truffles were listed as tubers, and if properly wrapped would pass inspection. We were about to leave when the Customs inspector plunged his hand once more into the bag and came up with an apple.

"And what is this?!"

"An apple," I whispered, feeling frightfully guilty—and with that the agent threw the apple into the garbage can. There went my lunch.

Clearly in America, it is truffles, yes! and apples, no!

That dinner lead to a conversation among Luciano, Mitchell Davis of the James Beard House, and me—reminiscing about risottos and how James Beard had written an article about rice in the December 1972 issue of "Gourmet". That article was probably the first time anyone of importance in the culinary world had taken notice of this little "side dish" (as described by James Beard). Luciano remembered preparing the traditional *Risotto alla Milanese* for Mr. Beard, followed by Risotto with Smoked Salmon, which James Beard renamed as Risotto Villa d'Este. In turn we changed the name to Risotto à la James Beard, and listed it in our menu at the Verandah Restaurant at Villa d'Este for years to come.

At that time, not many of our guests were familiar with the risotto dishes that are the mainstay of northern Italian cooking, but we kept on serving them, knowing that eventually risotto would be given its rightful place in the gourmet food world, with no small thanks to the efforts of Luciano Parolari, whose innovative and delicious creations with our signature regional dish have earned him the name "King of Risotto" both at home in Italy and abroad.

Now we find that many of our visitors, famous worldwide and to those of us at Villa d'Este, visit the hotel in part so they can partake of the wonderful risottos that come from our kitchens. Here we recount how to make them—and just as important, how this little "side dish" has created reverberations around the world!

We hope that our readers—visitors and non-visitors alike—glean just a small taste of Villa d'Este and the best risottos in the world from this book.

Jean Govoni Salvadore
Villa d'Este
Lake Como, Italy

Risotto with Scallops
and Risotto with Porcini
Mushrooms.

All You Need to Know

This book includes more than fifty recipes, along with all the basic information needed to make a perfect risotto. Some are classics and some are variations that we have invented or perfected over the years at Villa d'Este and are favorites of our guests. All of the recipes here can be prepared easily and most will cook in less than thirty minutes—twenty for the risotto and an additional ten or so for the add-ons.

The recipes are organized by main ingredients, except for a few that have been organized by the ideal season for their ingredients, that is, when they traditionally have been in season and available. Today, of course, almost all of the special ingredients are available to the cook year-round, but there was a time when artichokes, for example, were only available during the spring months; white truffles during the fall; and so on—so these were the only times we could make these specific risottos.

Risotto is a Milanese institution that was introduced to what is now Italy by the Saracens between the eighth and eleventh centuries. The dish has become a mainstay of northern Italy and today can be found on menus and family tables from Milan to Venice and Turin to Como.

Risotto is more than simply a technique for cooking rice, and to be authentic, it must be made from a particular variety of rice, called Carnaroli, which is indigenous to northern Italy. The provinces of Vercelli and Novara produce three-quarters of all the rice grown in Italy. This rice comes from the very fertile Po Valley of northern Italy, but can now be found in almost any in gourmet food shop and often in large supermarkets.

Carnaroli is longer grained than American rice, but what makes this rice special is its ability to absorb to an unusual degree the flavors from the ingredients that it is cooked with—it merges with the cooking liquid to create a consistency whereby each individual grain of rice remains firm and *al dente*. Also, Carnaroli rice doesn't get mushy if you slightly overcook it, and it will maintain its *al dente* texture better, longer, and easier than other types of rice. This combination of qualities is what makes risotto unique. The finished dish should be tender and creamy, not soft and mushy. Arborio rice can certainly be substituted for Carnaroli, but is has to be watched a little more carefully.

It is important to note that traditionally risotto has been a first course in the Italian meal—following the appetizer and preceding the main course. However, risotto can now be served as a main course. A basic risotto with just an addition of Parmesan, champagne, or saffron is generally served as a first course, but when served in combination with any type of meat, chicken, or shellfish, it can be served as a main course. Many diners, appreciating the luxury of a risotto, prefer to eat a single larger course.

Italians are known to have a flair for cooking because of their creativity in method and the variety of ingredients they use; for example, there are hundreds of ways to make even the most basic bolognese—also called ragù, or meat sauce. But for risotto there is one fundamental recipe that must be followed religiously—even when making variations.

The four basic steps in making a risotto are as follows: sautéing the onion with oil and/or butter until softened; adding the rice to the pan and stirring to coat until the grains are translucent; adding the stock about ½ cup at a time until completely absorbed by the rice; and, finally, stirring in the final elements—which always include butter, and usually cheese, plus any extra ingredients.

Quality ingredients are the key to a perfect risotto, and this important feature cannot be stressed strongly enough. For best results the broth should be homemade and barely salted. Tasting throughout the process is important—it may be that extra tablespoons of butter and Parmesan should be added at the last moment to enrich the risotto.

And it is important that the rice be Carnaroli (see above), and all the ingredients should be fresh. For example, the Parmesan cheese should be grated just before serving the risotto.

Traditionally risotto is made mostly with butter, but today many people prefer olive oil. If olive oil is used, it should be extra virgin—it is easier to digest and certainly healthier—and the best Italian oils are from the northern regions of Liguria (a light extra virgin oil) or Umbria (a medium extra virgin oil). Olive oils from the south of Italy tend to be too strong.

Always use a large saucepan with a heavy bottom for your risotto, heat the butter or olive oil, and sauté or sweat the onions until translucent. The rice should always be covered by a veil of broth when cooking and at the finish, as many risotto lovers ask for their risotto to be *all'onda* or "on the wave," meaning a bit moist. As a rule of thumb, the stock should be made from scratch for best results, although prepared stock may be used in an emergency. Chicken stock is the preferred liquid for making a risotto, but beef and fish stocks may also be used—and recipes for these are included here too.

When the risotto is cooked, the final touch is to *mantecare*, which literally means to pound the rice with butter (or oil) together with Parmesan cheese, which adds a great finish to the dish. This is done once the pan has been removed from the burner, and then the risotto should be left to rest for a few minutes before serving. The finished risotto should be soft and creamy, not soggy and mushy.

What is the favorite risotto of the guests at Villa d'Este? By far Risotto with Porcini Mushrooms steals the hearts and palates of all. The best time to enjoy the porcini is from September to November, although they can be found practically all year round, but at exorbitant prices when out of season. Available only in Italy, porcini mushrooms are now in great demand, so much so that many top Italian restaurants throughout the world—especially in the United States—have them imported. Many people who visit Italy purchase dried porcini mushrooms to bring home with them. Depending on various import regulations, the mushrooms are usually allowed to be carried out if firmly packaged and sealed. These dried porcini are ideal to use with risotto because they have a lovely strong taste and can be used in small quantities, which ensures just the right amount of subtle porcini taste.

Now you have in hand the basic information you need to create memorable risottos from this book—or to improvise and create some of your own. I have lived in the risotto region of Italy my entire life and continue to be delighted in the varieties I encounter and the imagination that can be brought to bear in cooking them. I hope that this book will inspire you—through not only its recipes, but through the wonderful stories of those who have loved risottos through the years at Villa d'Este—to do the same.

Luciano Parolari
Villa d'Este
Lake Como, Italy

No matter which risotto you are preparing, be sure to follow these important rules:

1 Do not overcook the rice—
the total cooking time should not exceed 20 minutes.

2 Do not wash the rice before cooking—
the starch is what makes the risotto creamy.

3 Maintain a constant cooking temperature by keeping the stock at a bare simmer as you cook the risotto.

Here are the recipes for the basic stocks, one of which will be used in every risotto:

Chicken or Beef Stock

Makes 2 ½ quarts

3 to 4 pound whole chicken or 2 pounds stewing beef
4 quarts cold water
1 tablespoon coarse salt
1 bay leaf
2 carrots, coarsely chopped
1 medium onion, chopped
1 leek, chopped
2 celery stalks

1 Place the chicken or beef in a large stockpot and cover with the water. Add the salt and bay leaf. Cover and slowly bring to a boil, skimming any foam with a slotted spoon. Add the carrots, onion, leek, and celery.

2 Bring back to a boil, then reduce the heat and simmer, uncovered, for 90 minutes, skimming the foam occasionally. Strain the broth through a fine-mesh sieve. Discard the solids.

3 If using the stock right away, skim off and discard the fat. If not, let cool, covered, then refrigerate. Remove the fat from the chilled stock. The stock may be refrigerated for a few days.

If you are freezing the stock, remove the chicken or beef and the vegetables. Leave the pot uncovered, increase the heat to high, and reduce the liquid by half. Let cool, then strain into containers and place in the freezer.

Fish Stock

Makes 6 cups

1 bay leaf
5 parsley sprigs
5 thyme sprigs
1 pound bones and trimmings of white fish
   (such as sole or turbot)
1 onion, coarsely chopped
1 carrot, coarsely chopped
1 celery stalk, coarsely chopped
1 leek, coarsely chopped
6 cups water
2 cups dry white wine
Salt and freshly ground black pepper to taste

1 Place the bay leaf, parsley, and thyme at the bottom of a large stockpot.
Cover with the fish bones and trimmings. Add the vegetables, water, and
wine. Bring to a boil, skimming off the foam. Reduce the heat and simmer,
uncovered, for 30 minutes.

2 Strain through a fine-mesh sieve. Discard the solids. Add salt and pepper
to taste. If not using the stock right away, cool completely, uncovered,
then refrigerate.

Vegetable Stock

Makes 2 ½ quarts

1/4 cup extra virgin olive oil
1 yellow onion, coarsely chopped
1 carrot, coarsely chopped
2 celery stalks, chopped, and whatever other vegetable
   may be available, except broccoli and cabbage
4 quarts water
1 bouquet garni

1 Heat the olive oil in a large stockpot over medium heat. Add the onion, carrot, celery and the vegetables and cook until starting to soften, about 5 minutes. Add cold water and bouquet garni. Bring to a boil, then reduce the heat and simmer, uncovered, for 30 minutes.

2 Strain through a fine-mesh sieve into a clean heatproof container, pressing down on the vegetables. Discard the solids. Cool completely, uncovered, then refrigerate.

A Note on Stock and Broth

The words stock and broth are often used interchangeably to describe the liquid made by cooking chicken, beef, fish, or vegetables in water for a few hours. Stock is commonly used to describe the liquid when it is homemade, while broth is a term more frequently applied to commercially made packages.

Fresh vegetables and herbs from the Villa d'Este kitchen garden.

Liquid or Volume Measures

Unit of measure	Equivalent measurement	Equivalent measurement
1 teaspoon		1/3 tablespoon
1 tablespoon	1/2 fluid ounce	3 teaspoons
2 tablespoons	1 fluid ounce	1/8 cup/6 teaspoons
1/4 cup	2 fluid ounces	4 tablespoons
1/3 cup	2 2/3 fluid ounces	5 tablespoons & 1 teaspoon
1/2 cup	4 fluid ounces	8 tablespoons
2/3 cup	5 1/3 fluid ounces	10 tablespoons & 2 teaspoons
3/4 cup	6 fluid ounces	12 tablespoons
7/8 cup	7 fluid ounces	14 tablespoons
1 cup	8 fluid ounces/1/2 pint	16 tablespoons
2 cups	16 fluid ounces/1 pint	32 tablespoons
4 cups	32 fluid ounces	1 quart
1 pint	16 fluid ounces/1 pint	32 tablespoons
2 pints	32 fluid ounces	1.0 quart
8 pints	1 gallon/128 fluid ounces	4 quarts
4 quarts	1 gallon/128 fluid ounces	8 pints
1 liter	1.057 quarts	
128 fluid ounces	1 gallon	

Unit of measure	Decimal equivalent	Metric measurement
1 teaspoon	.3333 tablespoon	5 ml
1 tablespoon	.5 fluid ounce	15 ml/ 15 cc
2 tablespoons	.125 cup	30 ml/30 cc
1/4 cup	.25 cup	59 ml
1/3 cup	.3333 cup	79 ml
1/2 cup	.5 cup	118 ml
2/3 cup	.6667 cup	158 ml
3/4 cup	.75 cup	177 ml
7/8 cup	.875 cup	207 ml
1 cup	1.0 cup	237 ml
2 cups	2.0 cup	473 ml
4 cups	4.0 cup	946 ml
1 pint	1.0 pint	473 ml
2 pints	1.0 quart	946 ml/0.946 liters
8 pints	1.0 gallon	3785 m/3.78 liters
4 quarts	1.0 gallon	3785 ml/3.78 liters
1 liter		1000 ml
128 fluid ounces		3785 ml/3.78 liters

Basic Conversions

Dry or Weight Measurements (approximate)

Unit of measure	Equivalent measurement	Decimal equivalent	Metric measurement
1 ounce	1/16 pound	.0625 pound	30 grams (28.35 g)
2 ounces	1/8 pound	.125 pound	55 grams
3 ounces	3/16 pound	.1875 pound	85 grams
4 ounces	1/4 pound	.250 pound	125 grams
8 ounces	1/2 pound	.5 pound	240 grams
12 ounces	3/4 pound	.75 pound	375 grams
16 ounces	1 pound	1.0 pound	454 grams
32 ounces	2 pounds	2.0 pounds	907 grams
1 kilogram	2.2 pounds/ 35.2 ounces	1000 grams	

The Veranda Restaurant, boasting the finest service and views, is easily enjoyed by any risotto lover.

Oven Temperature Equivalents

Centigrade	Fahrenheit	Heat
105	225	Very cool
120	250	
135	275	Cool
150	300	
160	325	Moderate
175	350	
190	375	Moderately hot
200	400	
222	425	Hot
230	450	
245	475	Very hot

Quick Reference Glossary of Ingredients and Terms

Here is a description of some of the terms used in the recipes that are crucial to making a perfect risotto.

Al Dente This literally means "to the tooth" and is used frequently in Italian cooking. It means that the rice or pasta has been cooked to the point that it is tender but still firm at its center, making it a little chewy.

Bouquet Garni A bundle of herbs usually added at the start of cooking to flavor a stock or soup.

Butter Unsalted is best.

Carnaroli Rice Longer grained than American rice, this is the perfect rice for cooking risotto. It has a particular ability to absorb the flavors of a risotto and doesn't get mushy if you slightly overcook it; it will keep its *al dente* texture longer and with more ease than any other rice. Arborio rice can be substituted if Carnaroli cannot be found.

Olive Oil One of the most important ingredients in making risotto, extra virgin olive oil is the highest grade of olive oil, extracted from the fruit without the use of heat or chemicals.

Parmesan Cheese This cheese is known by the name Parmigiano-Reggiano in most markets and is a firm, salty cheese made from cow's milk that comes from the Emilia-Romagna region of northern Italy.   It is best to buy whole chunks and grate the cheese just before serving the risotto.

Saffron This seasoning is an essential ingredient in the classic Risotto Milanese. It tints the risotto a beautiful shade of yellow and is highly aromatic. It is best to buy saffron in threads rather than ground saffron because the threads can be crushed just before using and will hold their flavor longer.

Stock/Broth The liquid used to keep the risotto moist throughout the cooking process. We use the two terms interchangeably. Stock can be made from scratch, as described on pages 22–27, or in an emergency prepared broth or bouillon cubes can be used. The stock that's added to risotto should be kept warm but not boiling; have it heating in a separate pan so that consistency of temperature is guaranteed while you're cooking.

Recipes

Risottos on the Lake by the famous
Floating pool: Clockwise from left, Risotto
with Radicchio and Smoked Provolone;
Risotto with Spring Vegetables; Risotto
with Perch Fillets; Risotto with Seafood;
Risotto with Porcini Mushrooms; Black
Squid Ink Risotto; Risotto with Asparagus.

Risotto with Four Cheeses
Risotto ai Quattro Formaggi

Men's fashion designer and stylist Eugene Venanzi and his wife, Anna, visit
Villa d'Este a couple of times a year. Since Anna is of Italian descent, she is
very much attached to her culinary traditions and takes her cooking seriously.
While she has tried every possible variety of Luciano's risottos, this one is
her favorite.

Serves 4 to 6

6 cups chicken stock
1 tablespoon butter
1 tablespoon extra virgin olive oil
1 small red onion, finely chopped
2 cups Carnaroli rice
2 ounces Taleggio cheese
2 ounces Fontina cheese
1 ounce Gorgonzola cheese
2 tablespoons grated Parmesan cheese
Salt and freshly ground black pepper to taste

1 Bring the stock to a boil in a medium saucepan, then reduce the heat
and keep at a bare simmer.

2 Melt the butter with the olive oil in a large, heavy saucepan over medium
heat. Add the onion and cook, stirring constantly with a wooden spoon, until
softened and translucent, about 3 minutes. Add the rice and cook, stirring,
for about 3 minutes, until every grain is coated with butter and oil.

3 Add 1 cup of the stock and stir until the liquid is absorbed. Continue
adding stock, about ½ cup at a time, stirring frequently and making sure
all the liquid is absorbed before adding more stock. Cook until the rice is
just tender and creamy but still *al dente*, 15 to 20 minutes. You may have
leftover stock.

4 Combine the four cheeses together in a bowl, and add them to the risotto.
Remove the pan from the heat and add salt and pepper to taste. Let the
risotto rest for a minute or two and serve immediately, piping hot.

Risotto with Gorgonzola Cheese
Risotto al Gorgonzola

Senior consulting editor for *Condé Nast Traveler*, professional connoisseur, gourmet, and traveler extraordinaire Clive Irving writes eloquently about his favorite risotto at Villa d'Este:

I had never experienced the joy of a Gorgonzola risotto until the early 1990s. Mimi, my wife, and I arrived early one morning at Malpensa airport in Milan, from New York. Malpensa had only just opened and was very full of *mal pensas*, having invented the world's finest machine for losing baggage. We were driving south into Piedmont, and needing a few strong shots of coffee to deal with our jet lag and our bad thoughts, we stopped in the small town of Moncalvo. It was market day.

There was a wonderful array of produce on display at the market. Among the Piedmont cheeses was a huge wheel of Gorgonzola. I had never seen Gorgonzola like it: Where the wheel had been cut, it presented a sheer cliff face of oozing, creamy cheese, interlaced with dark blue veins. I bought a small piece and we lapped it up like ice cream.

The night we stayed at the Locanda del Sant'Uffizio-da-Beppe, a cozy place run by Beppe Firato and his family in a hamlet called Cioccaro di Penango. Beppe had started life as a pork butcher, and his homemade salumi, of many kinds, was legendary. After sleeping off the jet lag, we had an enormous appetite. We ate a seven-course dinner, but the most memorable taste of the evening was the risotto—made with the same rich Gorgonzola we had found in the market. The rice, of course, had come from the nearby Po Valley.

We never thought we would find a risotto to equal the one we had that night, and we didn't—until a few years later when we arrived at Villa d'Este for our first visit, late in September. We discovered that Luciano revered and respected the Gorgonzola-rice connection as much as the Firato family, with whom we first experienced the epiphany of rice joined with Gorgonzola. That risotto was our first introduction to Luciano's brilliance and an indication of why he would come to be known as the "King of Risotto".

Drink a glass of good Sauterne with this risotto—something like a Doisy-Daëne rather than d'Yquem, which would be criminally frivolous!

The town of Gorgonzola, the home of the cheese of which Clive Irving speaks, is in the Lombardy region—the same region as Villa d'Este. This recipe was originally published in the May 1970 issue of *Gourmet* magazine.

Serves 4 to 6
6 cups chicken stock
3 tablespoons butter
1 small onion, finely chopped
2 cups Carnaroli rice
6 tablespoons Gorgonzola cheese
2 tablespoons heavy cream
3 medium tomatoes, peeled, seeded, and diced
1 tablespoon grated Parmesan cheese
Salt and freshly ground black pepper to taste

1 Bring the stock to a boil in a medium saucepan, then reduce the heat and keep at a bare simmer.

2 Melt 1 tablespoon of the butter in a large, heavy saucepan over medium heat. Add the onion and cook, stirring constantly with a wooden spoon, until softened and translucent, about 3 minutes. Add the rice and cook, stirring, for about 3 minutes, until every grain is coated with butter.

3 Add 1 cup of the stock and stir until the liquid is absorbed. Continue adding stock, about ½ cup at a time, stirring frequently and making sure all the liquid is absorbed before adding more stock. Cook until the rice is just tender and creamy but still *al dente*, 15 to 20 minutes. You may have leftover stock.

4 Combine the Gorgonzola cheese with the cream in a bowl. Remove the pan from the heat and stir in the Gorgonzola cheese mixture. Add the diced tomatoes, the remaining 2 tablespoons butter, the Parmesan cheese, and salt and pepper to taste. Let the risotto rest for a minute or two and serve piping hot.

Risotto with Parmesan Cheese
Risotto alla Parmigiana

Although Australian journalist and media professional Christine Hogan
was in her twenties before she tasted risotto, this was due in large part to
the fact that, as she explains, her hometown of Brisbane "lacked cuisine until
the 1970s." Now, of course, she knows better and waxes rhapsodic whenever
risotto is mentioned:

Since I was editing a food and wine section of a major daily newspaper, I
knew that a risotto included rice and meant a lot of trouble over the stove—
but the rest was a mystery. I'm not even too sure I had heard the word
pronounced properly until my host, Luca Salvadore, recommended *Risotto
alla Milanese* from the menu at Villa d'Este.

I accepted Luca's advice, and out of the kitchen and onto the table came a
plate of golden, succulent Carnaroli rice, cooked perfectly (as I now know)
and with just a hint of crispness still in the grains. That saffron risotto was an
epiphany, but it was also a honey-colored trap, and here's why: The first time
you taste risotto and it is at the Villa d'Este from a recipe by Chef Luciano
Parolari, where is there to go after that?

I have now tried risottos across the world, and even occasionally make
them in my own kitchen in Sydney, but the place I go to repeat that first
unforgettable experience is, of course, Villa d'Este. Every time I am fortunate
enough to be there, I ask the wonderful Eugenio in the formal Verandah
Restaurant for the Champagne Risotto at lunch. One night, when I was
feeling a little off color, he suggested *Risotto in Bianco*—it was then I
discovered that with a little butter and a little Parmesan cheese, *Risotto
alla Parmigiana* was the luxury end of comfort food!

Serves 4 to 6
6 cups chicken stock
4 tablespoons butter
1 tablespoon extra virgin olive oil
1 small onion, finely chopped
2 cups Carnaroli rice
6 tablespoons grated Parmesan cheese, plus more for serving
½ cup sparkling wine
Salt and freshly ground black pepper to taste

1 Bring the stock to a boil in a medium saucepan, then reduce the heat and keep at a bare simmer.

2 Melt 1 tablespoon of the butter with the olive oil in a large, heavy saucepan over medium heat. Add the onion and cook, stirring constantly with a wooden spoon, until softened and translucent, about 3 minutes. Add the rice and cook, stirring, for about 3 minutes, until every grain is coated with butter and oil.

3 Add 1 cup of the stock and stir until the liquid is absorbed. Continue adding stock, about ½ cup at a time, stirring frequently and making sure all the liquid is absorbed before adding more stock. Cook until the rice is just tender and creamy but still *al dente*, 15 to 20 minutes. You may have leftover stock.

4 Remove the pan from the heat and stir in the remaining 3 tablespoons butter, the Parmesan cheese, sparkling wine, and salt and pepper to taste. Let the risotto rest for a minute or two and serve piping hot, with additional Parmesan on the side.

Risotto with Veal Meatballs and Fontina Cheese Fondue

Risotto con Morbidelle di Vitello e Fonduta di Fontina

A young visitor named Chip Morrison, aged thirteen, writes:

Risotto and Me:
A Young Person's Point of View

❝I first visited Villa d'Este when I was six years old. Even then, I was impressed and mesmerized by the lobby's artwork and architecture. Even more impressive, though, was the terrace of our room, which overlooked the lake. Little did I know the trip was about to get better.

It was just dusk when we went to the formal Verandah to eat. I opened the menu and started to scan it, eventually settling on the Black and White Fettuccini Alfredo. My mom ordered veal, and my dad ordered something called risotto. I thought to myself, "What could this risotto be?" When our food arrived, dad asked me if I wanted to try some risotto. I thought, "Oh well, trying out new things isn't bad." I took a small bite, and wow! "Man," I said to my parents, "I've never tasted something sooooo . . . good."

My mother said, "So I take it you like it."

"I love it!" I guess that is when my obsession for risotto started.

Ever since, it has become a birthday tradition for my mother to order duck and for me to order Black and White Fettuccini Alfredo with a side order of risotto. (My mother and I have the same birthday.) No matter how many times I order the risotto, each one gets better. I am now thirteen and my plans from here on out are to keep going to Villa d'Este and eating risotto.❞

Serves 4 to 6

Fontina Cheese Fondue

9 ounces Fontina cheese, cut into cubes
½ cup milk
1 egg yolk

Veal Meatballs

9 ounces veal, trimmed of fat
½ cup white bread pieces
1 slice white bread, removed of crust
2 tablespoons milk
2 tablespoons grated Parmesan cheese
1 small onion, finely chopped
Salt and freshly ground black pepper to taste
2 tablespoons butter
2 sage leaves

Risotto

6 cups chicken stock
1 tablespoon butter
2 tablespoons extra virgin olive oil
1 small onion, thinly sliced
2 cups Carnaroli rice
½ cup dry white wine
Salt and freshly ground black pepper to taste

1 Place the Fontina cheese in a bowl. Cover with the milk and soak for 2 hours.

2 Place the bread for the meatballs in another bowl. Cover with the milk and soak for about 3 minutes.

3 To make the meatballs, grind the meat fine, then crumble and add the soaked bread, along with the Parmesan cheese, onion, and salt and pepper to taste. Mix well using your hands.

4 Roll the mixture into meatballs a little smaller than golf balls.

5 Melt the butter in a large skillet over medium-high heat. Add the sage. Brown the meatballs on all sides. Keep warm while you're making the risotto.

6 Meanwhile make the risotto: Bring the stock to a boil in a medium saucepan, then reduce the heat and keep at a bare simmer.

7 Melt the butter with the olive oil in a large, heavy saucepan over medium heat. Add the onion and cook, stirring constantly with a wooden spoon, until softened and translucent, about 3 minutes. Add the rice and cook, stirring, for about 3 minutes, until every grain is coated with butter and oil. Then add the wine and stir until absorbed.

8 Add 1 cup of the stock and stir until the liquid is absorbed. Continue adding stock, about ½ cup at a time, stirring frequently and making sure all the liquid is absorbed before adding more stock. Cook until the rice is just tender and creamy but still *al dente*, 15 to 20 minutes. You may have leftover stock.

9 Just before the risotto is finished, make the fondue: Place the soaked Fontina cheese in the top of a double boiler placed over simmering water. Heat for about 5 to 10 minutes, until the ingredients are well amalgamated and you have a thick consistency. Add the egg yolk and mix well until creamy.

10 Remove the risotto pan from the heat and add salt and pepper to taste Let the risotto rest for a minute or two and serve piping hot, topped with the meatballs and fondue.

Risotto with Apples
Risotto con le Mele

Ellen Sweeney, a travel expert on all things Villa d'Este, Como, and
Cernobbio, has been visiting the region for thirteen years. Besides falling in
love with the Italian landscape, people, and culture, she adores the cuisine,
especially Luciano's Risotto with Apples. The tangy, sweet crunch of the
apples might seem to clash with the creamy flavor of the risotto, but the
reverse is true. The unique combination infuses the dish with a delicious
and distinct taste, creating a symphony out of opposing flavors.

Serves 4 to 6
4 tablespoons butter
2 crisp apples, peeled and very thinly sliced
Pinch of cinnamon
¼ cup Calvados
6 cups chicken stock
1 tablespoon extra virgin olive oil
1 small onion, finely chopped
2 cups Carnaroli rice
6 tablespoons diced Taleggio cheese
½ cup sparkling white wine
Salt and freshly ground black pepper to taste

1 Heat 1 tablespoon of the butter in a medium sauté pan, add the apples
and cinnamon, and sauté for 3 minutes, until the apples are soft but still
hold their shape. Flame with the Calvados and set aside.

2 Bring the stock to a boil in a medium saucepan, then reduce the heat and
keep at a bare simmer.

3 Melt 1 tablespoon of the butter with the olive oil in a large, heavy
saucepan over medium heat. Add the onion and cook, stirring constantly
with a wooden spoon, until softened and translucent, about 3 minutes. Add
the rice and cook, stirring, for about 3 minutes, until every grain is coated
with butter and oil.

4 Add 1 cup of the stock and stir until the liquid is absorbed. Continue adding stock, about ½ cup at a time, stirring frequently and making sure all the liquid is absorbed before adding more stock. Cook until the rice is just tender and creamy but still *al dente*, 15 to 20 minutes. You may have leftover stock.

5 Remove the pan from the heat and stir in the remaining 2 tablespoons butter, the Taleggio cheese, sparkling wine, and salt and pepper to taste. Add the apples and stir well. Let the risotto rest for a minute or two and serve piping hot.

Risotto with Artichokes
Risotto con Carciofi

This is a risotto that for many years could only be made during the artichoke season, which is the month of March. That was true in the days when Frank Sinatra and Ava Gardner visited Villa d'Este. Of course Frank was of Italian descent, but he hadn't actually visited Italy until he came to Villa d'Este. At this point he was too famous to travel incognito, so he needed a place like Villa d'Este to which he could retreat in comfort. Add to that the brewing scandal with Ava Gardner, and he had very few options—especially if he wanted to visit Italy.

So during the early 1950s they arrived in a flurry at Villa d'Este ready to partake of Italian fare. They were offered risotto at the formal Verandah Restaurant—the staff wanted to make sure they had an authentic northern Italian experience. Sinatra was dubious; Gardner was willing—so the very special seasonal Risotto with Artichokes was prepared and offered in a formal flourish.

The diners were ecstatic. Who could not love *Risotto con Carciofi*? In fact, from that time on when Sinatra returned (always, alas, sans Gardner) he made sure to make his first stop the formal Verandah and his first bite *Risotto con Carciofi*!

Serves 4 to 6

6 artichoke hearts

4½ tablespoons butter

2 tablespoons extra virgin olive oil

6 cups chicken stock

1 small onion, finely chopped

2 cups Carnaroli rice

1 cup Italian spumante (sparkling wine)

3 tablespoons grated Parmesan cheese

Salt and freshly ground black pepper to taste

1 tablespoon minced flat-leaf parsley

1 Cut the artichokes into very thin slices. Set aside half of the slices. Melt ½ tablespoon of the butter with 1 tablespoon of the olive oil in a medium sauté pan over medium heat. Add the artichokes and sauté for 3 minutes, or until soft in the center. Set aside.

2 Bring the stock to a boil in a medium saucepan, then reduce the heat and keep at a bare simmer.

3 Melt 1 tablespoon of the butter with the remaining 1 tablespoon olive oil in a large, heavy saucepan over medium heat. Add the onion and cook, stirring constantly with a wooden spoon, until softened and translucent, about 3 minutes. Add the rice and cook, stirring, for about 3 minutes, until every grain is coated with butter and oil. Then add ½ cup of the spumante and stir until absorbed.

4 Add 1 cup of the stock and stir until the liquid is absorbed. Add the uncooked sliced artichokes. Continue adding stock, about ½ cup at a time, stirring frequently and making sure all the liquid is absorbed before adding more stock. Cook until the rice is just tender and creamy but still *al dente*, 15 to 20 minutes. You may have leftover stock.

Risotto with Artichokes.

5 Add the remaining ½ cup of the spumante and stir will. Remove the pan from the heat and stir in the remaining 3 tablespoons butter, the Parmesan cheese, and salt and pepper to taste.

6 Let the risotto rest for a minute or two and serve on individual plates, topped with the sautéed artichokes and a sprinkling of the parsley. This risotto can also be served with any kind of Italian sausage, either grilled or sautéed with sage and butter.

Risotto with Asparagus
Risotto agli Asparagi

Frequent guest, aficionado of all things Italian, and well-known literary guru and editor Larry Ashmead says this is his favorite of Luciano's recipes. The secret to this recipe is the asparagus. With just enough of a satisfying crunch, it counteracts the creamy rice, creating a perfectly balanced texture—one that, in Larry's mind, simply cannot be rivalled.

Serves 4 to 6
6 cups chicken stock
4 tablespoons butter
1 tablespoon extra virgin olive oil
1 small onion, thinly sliced
2 cups Carnaroli rice
42 asparagus tips, parboiled
1 tablespoon grated Parmesan cheese
4 tablespoons grated provola affumicata
   (smoked provola cheese)
Salt and freshly ground black pepper to taste

1 Bring the stock to a boil in a medium saucepan, then reduce the heat and keep at a bare simmer.

2 Melt 1 tablespoon of the butter with the olive oil in a large, heavy saucepan over medium heat. Add the onion and cook, stirring constantly with a

wooden spoon, until softened and translucent, about 3 minutes. Add the rice and cook, stirring, for about 3 minutes, until every grain is coated with butter and oil.

3 Add 1 cup of the stock and stir until the liquid is absorbed. Continue adding stock, about ½ cup at a time, stirring frequently and making sure all the liquid is absorbed before adding more stock. Halfway through cooking the risotto, add 24 of the asparagus tips, leaving the rest for garnish. Continue to add stock. Cook until the rice is just tender and creamy but still *al dente*, 15 to 20 minutes. You may have leftover stock. Remove the pan from the heat and stir in the remaining 3 tablespoons butter, the Parmesan cheese, provola, and salt and pepper to taste.

4 Let the risotto rest for a minute or two and serve on individual plates, each garnished with 3 asparagus tips.

Risotto with Celery
Risotto con Sedano

Former Como resident and fashion stylist Alvin Karstensen confesses that his favorite risotto was handed down to him by his friend and magazine publisher Fred Smith. When Luciano saw the recipe for Risotto with Celery, he decided to try it out but omitted the garlic because he thought the garlic would compete with the flavor of the celery. The procedure is more or less the same as a basic risotto, but with an added twist.

Serves 4 to 6
5 tablespoons butter
8 celery stalks, cut into small cubes (6 to 8 ounces)
1 clove garlic, chopped (optional)
½ teaspoon red pepper flakes
6 cups vegetable stock
2 tablespoons extra virgin olive oil
1 small onion, finely chopped
2 cups Carnaroli rice
3 tablespoons grated Parmesan cheese
Salt and freshly ground black pepper to taste

1 Warm 1 tablespoon of the butter in a medium skillet over medium heat. Add the celery, garlic, and red pepper flakes and sauté for about 5 minutes, or until the celery has begun to soften. Set aside.

2 Bring the stock to a boil in a medium saucepan, then reduce the heat and keep at a bare simmer.

3 Melt 1 tablespoon of the butter with 1 tablespoon of the olive oil in a large, heavy saucepan over medium heat. Add the onion and cook, stirring constantly with a wooden spoon, until softened and translucent, about 3 minutes. Add the rice and cook, stirring, for about 3 minutes, until every grain is coated with butter and oil.

4 Add 1 cup of the stock and stir until the liquid is absorbed. Continue adding stock, about ½ cup at a time, stirring frequently and making sure all the liquid is absorbed before adding more stock. Halfway through cooking the risotto, add the reserved celery mixture. Continue to add stock. Cook until the rice is just tender and creamy but still *al dente*, 15 to 20 minutes. You may have leftover stock.

5 Remove the pan from the heat and stir in the remaining 3 tablespoons butter, remaining 1 tablespoon olive oil, the Parmesan cheese, and salt and pepper to taste. Let the risotto rest for a minute or two and serve piping hot.

Risotto with Champagne
Risotto con Champagne

From the days when racing greats such as Jackie Stewart, James Hill, Niki Lauda, and Alain Prost became regular guests of Villa d'Este to more recent times when Michael Schumacher would fly back and forth between the hotel and the Grand Prix Monza Circuit, home of the annual Formula One car race, Luciano's risotto dishes have been in popular demand by these types of thrill-seekers.

Alain Prost found the risotto to be both delicious and a harbinger of good luck. He had the Milanese Risotto the night before entering the big Grand Prix race, and after that he never changed the order.

Niki Lauda always ordered Risotto with Champagne. Because he would be racing the next day, the kitchen staff knew to go light on the alcohol. But Lauda would still rush into the kitchen just to be sure the chef would sprinkle a small amount of champagne over the risotto.

This recipe is perfect for any kind of celebratory occasion—like being in the winner's circle of the Formula One!

The following story shows just how much this recipe is adored: A very elegant American gentleman arrived in the Villa d'Este dining room, alone, for lunch. When waiter extraordinaire Eugenio appeared to take the gentleman's order, the gentleman asked if Risotto with Champagne was on the menu. Sadly, it was not. The gentleman explained that he was in the region only for the day and had wanted to indulge in his favorite risotto. Eugenio slipped into the kitchen and explained the situation to Chef Luciano, who happily prepared the meal. Not only does Risotto with Champagne beckon diners from all corners of the Earth, but the Villa d'Este staff is dedicated to making sure that everyone—no matter the time or season—can repeatedly sample their favorite meals, even if it's as a special order.

Serves 4 to 6
6 cups chicken stock
4 tablespoons butter
1 small onion, finely chopped
2 cups Carnaroli rice
2 cups champagne
2 tablespoons grated Parmesan cheese
Salt and freshly ground black pepper to taste

1 Bring the stock to a boil in a medium saucepan, then reduce the heat and keep at a bare simmer.

2 Melt 1 tablespoon of the butter in a large, heavy saucepan over medium heat. Add the onion and cook, stirring constantly with a wooden spoon, until softened and translucent, about 3 minutes. Add the rice and cook, stirring, for about 3 minutes, until every grain is coated with butter and oil. Then add 1 ½ cups of the champagne and stir until absorbed.

3 Add 1 cup of the stock and stir until the liquid is absorbed. Continue adding stock, about ½ cup at a time, stirring frequently and making sure all the liquid is absorbed before adding more stock. Cook until the rice is just tender and creamy but still *al dente*, 15 to 20 minutes. You may have leftover stock. Add the remaining ½ cup champagne.

4 Remove the pan from the heat and stir in the remaining 3 tablespoons butter, the Parmesan cheese, and salt and pepper to taste. Let the risotto rest for a minute or two and serve piping hot.

Risotto with Lentils
Risotto con le Lenticchie

According to Italian tradition, lentils are served on New Year's Eve after midnight, and the more you eat the richer you become. With that in mind, it would be hard to imagine that there would be any lentils left in all of Italy. However my daughter, Claudia, passed her recipe for Risotto with Leftover Lentils to Luciano, who, with his magic touch, transformed it into a Villa d'Este New Year's favorite.

Serves 4 to 6
6 cups vegetable stock
4 tablespoons butter
1 tablespoon extra virgin olive oil
1 small onion, finely chopped
2 cups Carnaroli rice
½ pound pancetta or bacon, diced
⅓ pound lentils, boiled (or use the lentil recipe that follows)
4 tablespoons grated Parmesan cheese
Salt and freshly ground black pepper to taste

1 Bring the stock to a boil in a medium saucepan, then reduce the heat and keep at a bare simmer.

2 Melt 1 tablespoon of the butter with the olive oil in a large, heavy saucepan over medium heat. Add the onion and cook, stirring constantly with a wooden spoon, until softened and translucent, about 3 minutes. Add the rice and cook, stirring, for about 3 minutes, until every grain is coated with butter and oil.

3 Add 1 cup of the stock and stir until the liquid is absorbed. Continue adding stock, about ½ cup at a time, stirring frequently and making sure all the liquid is absorbed before adding more stock. Cook until the rice is just tender and creamy but still *al dente*, 15 to 20 minutes. You may have leftover stock.

4 While the risotto is cooking, cook the pancetta in a medium skillet over medium-high heat until crisp. Remove from the pan and drain on paper towels. Set aside.

5 Just before removing the risotto from the heat, add the lentils and pancetta.

6 Remove the risotto from the heat and stir in the remaining 3 tablespoons butter, the Parmesan cheese, and salt and pepper to taste. Let the risotto rest for a minute or two and serve piping hot.

Lentils

1 tablespoon extra virgin olive oil
3½ ounces pancetta or bacon, cut into small cubes
3 to 4 ounces Italian sausage (with or without garlic),
    casings removed and crumbled
2 sage leaves
3 ounces carrots, cut into small cubes
3 ounces onion, cut into small cubes
3 ounces celery, cut into small cubes
1 cup dry white wine
3 ounces plum tomatoes, cut into cubes
18 ounces lentils from Castelluccio (or other small lentils)
2 basil leaves, minced
Salt and freshly ground black pepper to taste

1 Warm the oil in a large saucepan over medium-high heat. Add the pancetta, crumbled sausage, and sage leaves and cook for about 5 minutes, until crisp. Add the carrots, onion, and celery and cook for about 5 minutes, until softened. Add the wine and stir to deglaze the pan. Add the tomatoes and lentils. Cover with water, raise the heat to high, and bring to a boil. Reduce the heat and simmer until all water is absorbed, adding more water if needed, until the lentils have softened but are still *al dente*. Cooking time varies from 30 minutes to 1 hour, depending on the quality of the lentils. Add the basil and salt and pepper to taste.

Risotto with Leftovers
Risotto con Avanzi

Even the best recipes can be discovered by accident. Remember the painter and his saffron? Magazine editor Richard Story chanced upon his favorite risotto by accidental resourcefulness:

Three summers ago, we visited our friends Ted and Eileen Pettus in Bridgehampton. They are both fantastic cooks—Ted on the grill, Eileen everywhere. Before we were to depart on Sunday evening, I said I'd make an early supper from leftovers. So I opened the refrigerator and here's what I found: a wedge of Brie, a container of vegetables (zucchini, eggplant, corn, and red, yellow, and orange peppers) that had been grilled the night before and served with a wonderful leg of lamb. Luckily, there was also Carnaroli rice, chicken stock, and a bottle of white wine. Oh, and I forgot the grilled onions. What could I make? A risotto, of course!

So I poured olive oil into the skillet, added a handful of the grilled onions, which I had finely chopped and sautéed for about five, maybe six minutes. Then I started adding the rice, slowly and carefully, like you're supposed to do when making risotto. On another burner, I heated a couple of cups of chicken stock and added white wine, which I ladled into the skillet in your typical risotto-making fashion. But the pièce de résistance was the vegetables, which I had chopped into very, very fine pieces—about a cup's worth—and the Brie, which I had also cut into tiny bits. About four minutes before the rice was fully cooked, I added the vegetables and Brie. The result was fantastic.

I am not what you would call a fastidious or even a precise cook. In other words, if a recipe calls for a half cup . . . well, why not whatever's left in the bottle? So what if it's a cup? And though the recipe calls for prosciutto, wouldn't turkey work just as well? You kind of get the idea of what sort of gourmet I am. That's not to say that I don't love wonderful cooking and understand that in many cases, precision and scientific expertise is essential. It's just that it's not my style, and that's how I created my masterpiece. . . purely by accident!

Any good chef has had his share of accidents in the kitchen, and Luciano is no exception. Here's his version of Richard's Risotto:

Serves 4 to 6
1 tablespoon extra virgin olive oil
½ cup finely chopped grilled onions
6 cups chicken stock
1½ cups Carnaroli rice
1 cup dry white wine
1 cup very finely chopped cooked vegetables
   (such as zucchini, eggplant, corn, and bell peppers)
¼ pound Brie, chopped into bits
Salt and freshly ground black pepper to taste

1 Warm the olive oil in a large, heavy saucepan over medium heat. Add the grilled onions and sauté for 5 to 6 minutes, until translucent.

2 Meanwhile, bring the stock to a boil in a medium saucepan, then reduce the heat and keep at a bare simmer.

3 Add the rice to the onions and cook, stirring, until every grain is coated with oil. Then add the wine and stir until absorbed.

4 Add 1 cup of the stock and stir until the liquid is absorbed. Continue adding stock, about ½ cup at a time, stirring frequently and making sure all the liquid is absorbed before adding more stock. About 4 minutes before the end of cooking time, add the vegetables and Brie. Continue to add stock. Cook until the rice is just tender and creamy but still *al dente*, 15 to 20 minutes. You may have leftover stock. Remove the pan from the heat and add salt and pepper to taste. Let the risotto rest for a minute or two and serve piping hot.

Risotto with Nettles
Risotto alle Ortiche

In addition to their good taste, nettles, an herbaceous plant commonly used in Italian cooking, are rich in vitamins A and C and are amazingly high in protein. This recipe is a transport from the region of Tuscany, where it is beloved, and Luciano has adapted the recipe in the Lombardy style. It is a favorite of writer Walter Matthews, who was a visitor to the hotel and a part-time resident of Tuscany.

Serves 4 to 6

6 cups chicken stock
4 tablespoons butter
2 tablespoons extra virgin olive oil
1 small onion, finely chopped
2 cups Carnaroli rice
6 tablespoons grated Parmesan cheese
1 cup sparkling white wine
8 ounces parboiled nettles, coarsely chopped
Salt and freshly ground black pepper to taste

1 Bring the stock to a boil in a medium saucepan, then reduce the heat and keep at a bare simmer.

2 Melt 2 tablespoons of the butter with 1 tablespoon of the olive oil in a large, heavy saucepan over medium heat. Add the onion and cook, stirring constantly with a wooden spoon, until softened and translucent, about 3 minutes. Add the rice and cook, stirring, for about 3 minutes, until every grain is coated with butter and oil.

3 Add 1 cup of the stock and stir until the liquid is absorbed. Add nettles. Continue adding stock, about ½ cup at a time, stirring frequently and making sure all the liquid is absorbed before adding more stock. Cook until the rice is just tender and creamy but still *al dente*, 15 to 20 minutes. You may have leftover stock.

4 Remove the pan from the heat and stir in the remaining 2 tablespoons butter, 1 tablespoon olive oil, the Parmesan cheese, and wine. Salt and pepper to taste and stir well. Let the risotto rest for a minute or two and serve piping hot.

Risotto with Green Peas and Prosciutto
Risotto con i Piselli e Prosciutto

Though travel writers Alexandra Mayes Birnbaum and her late husband Stephen tried countless risottos over the years, each recipe expertly prepared by Luciano, this is their favorite. And who can blame them? The saltiness of the prosciutto is balanced by the sweetness of the peas, making the finished dish a culinary masterpiece.

Serves 4
5 cups chicken stock
4 tablespoons butter
½ cup finely chopped onion
1½ cups Carnaroli rice
½ cup dry white wine
1 cup green peas
2 ounces sliced prosciutto, cut crosswise into ½ inch wide strips
1 teaspoon finely grated lemon zest
1 cup finely grated Parmesan cheese
3 tablespoons finely chopped flat-leaf parsley
Salt and freshly ground black pepper to taste

1 Bring the stock to a boil in a medium saucepan, then reduce the heat and keep at a bare simmer.

2 Melt 2 tablespoons of the butter in a large, heavy saucepan over medium heat. Add the onion and cook, stirring constantly with a wooden spoon, until softened and translucent, about 3 minutes. Add the rice and cook, stirring, for about 3 minutes, until every grain is coated with butter. Then add the wine and stir until absorbed.

3 Add 1 cup of the stock and the peas and stir until the liquid is absorbed. Continue adding stock, about ½ cup at a time, stirring frequently and making sure all the liquid is absorbed before adding more stock. Cook until the rice is just tender and creamy but still *al dente*, 15 to 20 minutes. You may have leftover stock.

4 Remove the pan from the heat and stir in prosciutto, lemon zest, remaining 2 tablespoons butter, ⅔ cup of the Parmesan cheese, the parsley, and salt and pepper to taste. Let the risotto rest for a minute or two and serve piping hot, topped with the remaining ⅓ cup Parmesan cheese.

Risotto with Porcini Mushrooms
Risotto con i Funghi Porcini

Next on our tour of risottos is a recipe that, by all accounts, seems to be the favorite of most visitors to Villa d'Este. This may have something to do with the fact that this risotto does not have a long list of ingredients. There is, however, one very special ingredient: porcini mushrooms.

The best time to enjoy the porcini mushroom is from September to November. However, they can be found practically all year round (at exorbitant prices!). They are available fresh only in Italy but, since they are in great demand, a few top Italian restaurants in New York City have the porcini shipped to the United States. Many of the Villa d'Este guests purchase dried porcini, which can be brought into the United States without incident if firmly packaged and sealed. Frequent visitor Valerie Heller, for example, admits to always buying a supply to last until her next visit because Risotto with Porcini was the favorite of her husband, Joseph Heller.

To give you an idea of how highly regarded this particular recipe is, we've included the following ode, "Risotto and Tears," written by Mary Rossi:

"How were we to know that Chef Luciano didn't cook risotto on Tuesdays?!

We had left Sydney thirty hours earlier and Theo, my husband, had kept up on a non-stop monologue in flight about how he could already taste the creamy richness of Parolari's signature dish. On arrival, Luca and Giovanna Salvadore took us straight into the splendid Verandah dining room. "A menu isn't necessary for us," we declared. "*Risotto con i funghi, per favor.*"

Our waiter understood perfectly and gently suggested, "*Domani sera*" for the risotto and, instead, the "*Crespelle di Magro per stasera.*" Great . . . my favorite, anyway.

But shock waves were felt at the table. It took a minute before I realized that the disturbed reaction was not emanating from Theo but from La Signora Salvadore. (In Australia, Giovanna has been given this title as though it indicates European royalty.) Her sense of Italian hospitality was under attack. She didn't understand why the whole of the Villa d'Este kitchen wouldn't come to a grinding halt to accommodate this mis-timed request for risotto.

When crêpes, not risotto, arrived at the table, it proved too much for La Signora. She left the table in tears. Although we didn't lose our appetites that night, there was one permanent result: There has never been another Tuesday night when risotto was not on the menu at Villa d'Este! La Signora insists that we note that this happened thirty-five years ago and was well before Luciano became the head chef, and the executive chef at the time was French.

Carla Porta Musa is a legend in Como, and nobody can believe that she is more than 100 years old. She is a poet and author of several books, including a cookbook, and she writes a weekly column for the local newspaper. Her house is frequented by writers and local intelligentsia. She always celebrates her birthday, March 15th, at Villa d'Este. She, too, prefers Risotto with Porcini Mushrooms above all the delicious possibilities."

As one last endorsement of the sublime nature of this risotto, devoted fan Shelley Stevens writes the following:

As you are aware, Luciano has attempted on several occasions to teach me the secrets of his famed risotto—but alas, only the maestro's touch will do! I know everyone's favorite risotto must be porcini, but I must tell you a funny story: When Luciano was in Dallas spreading his magic for a charity fundraiser, we went together to buy the ingredients for his world-renowned "food for the gods." He had planned porcini with Parmesan, but when we arrived at the produce area, I almost had to pick him up off the floor. The sign read porcini mushrooms: $57.99 per pound. Needless to say, we reluctantly moved on to the zucchini and Texas-grown mushrooms. Luciano, of course, did not miss a beat and, using the substitute local ingredients, the risotto was superb! It doesn't matter what Luciano is cooking—every recipe becomes a new favorite. (What? Did I hear white truffles? I can smell them being shaved in Luciano's kitchen just now. Yes! I am on my way.)

If you want to invite Shelley Stevens, Carla Porta Musa, or Mary Rossi to dinner, you will make them very happy by preparing this dish.

Serves 4 to 6
2 tablespoons extra virgin olive oil
1 clove garlic, chopped (optional)
1 cup fresh porcini mushrooms, washed, dried, and thinly sliced
6 cups chicken stock
3 tablespoons butter
1 small onion, finely chopped
2 cups Carnaroli rice
1 cup dry white wine
3 tablespoons grated Parmesan cheese, plus more for serving
Sprinkle of sparkling wine
1 tablespoon minced flat-leaf parsley
Salt and freshly ground black pepper to taste

1 Warm the olive oil in a small skillet over medium heat. Add the garlic and cook for 3 minutes. Add the mushrooms and sauté for 2 minutes, until softened but still firm.

2 Meanwhile, bring the stock to a boil in a medium saucepan, then reduce the heat and keep at a bare simmer.

3 Melt 2 tablespoons of the butter in a large, heavy saucepan over medium heat. Add the onion and cook, stirring constantly with a wooden spoon, until softened and translucent, about 3 minutes. Add half the sautéed mushrooms. 4 Then add the rice and cook, stirring, for about 3 minutes, until every grain is coated with butter. Then add the dry white wine and stir until absorbed.

5 Add 1 cup of the stock and stir until the liquid is absorbed. Continue adding stock, about ½ cup at a time, stirring frequently and making sure all the liquid is absorbed before adding more stock. Cook until the rice is just tender and creamy but still *al dente*, 15 to 20 minutes. You may have leftover stock.

6 Remove the pan from the heat and stir in the remaining 1 tablespoon butter, the Parmesan cheese, and sparkling wine. Season with salt and pepper to taste. Let the risotto rest for a minute or two and serve topped with the remaining sautéed mushrooms, the parsley, and a sprinkle of Parmesan cheese.

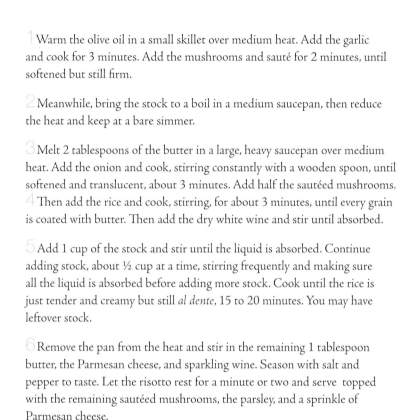

Risotto with Potatoes and Garlic
Risotto con Patate e Aglio

Family friend and chef Julia Smith created this recipe and Luciano perfected it.

Serves 4 to 6
2 tablespoons plus 1 teaspoon extra virgin olive oil
4 potatoes, cut into small cubes
Salt and freshly ground black pepper to taste
Splash of white wine
1 pound fresh baby spinach leaves
6 cups chicken stock
2 tablespoons butter
1 small yellow onion, diced
2 celery stalks, diced
5 cloves garlic, minced
2 cups Carnaroli rice
½ teaspoon saffron threads
⅓ cup grated Parmesan cheese
Chopped chives, for garnish

1 Warm 1 tablespoon of the olive oil in a large sauté pan over medium heat. Add the potatoes, season with salt and pepper, and cook for about 5 minutes, until the potatoes are lightly browned. Add a splash of wine. Allow it to evaporate and continue to cook for 5 more minutes. Remove from the pan and set aside.

2 Wipe the sauté pan clean with a paper towel and add 1 teaspoon of the olive oil to lightly coat the pan. Add the spinach, season with salt and pepper, and cook until the spinach is barely wilted, about 5 minutes. Remove the spinach from the pan and set aside.

3 Meanwhile, bring the stock to a boil in a medium saucepan, then reduce the heat and keep at a bare simmer.

4 Melt 1 tablespoon of the butter with the remaining 1 tablespoon olive oil in a large, heavy saucepan over medium heat. Add the onion and celery and sauté for 2 minutes. Add the garlic and continue to sauté until the onions are translucent, another minute or two. Add the rice and cook, stirring, for about 3 minutes, until every grain is coated with butter and oil.

5 Add the saffron and 1 cup of the stock and stir until the liquid is absorbed. Continue adding stock, about ½ cup at a time, stirring frequently and making sure all the liquid is absorbed before adding more stock. After 5 minutes add the potatoes and the spinach

6 Cook until the rice is just tender and creamy but still *al dente*, 15 to 20 minutes. You may have leftover stock. Remove the pan from the heat and stir in the remaining 1 tablespoon butter, the Parmesan cheese, and salt and pepper to taste. Let the risotto rest for a minute or two and serve piping hot, garnished with the chives.

Risotto with Radicchio and Smoked Provolone Cheese
Risotto con Radicchio e Provola Affumicata

When Bill Blass first started visiting Italy in the 1960s, he was intrigued by radicchio, which was impossible to find in the States, even in New York, except at very specialized markets.

On one visit to Villa d'Este, Bill Blass's waiter at the Verandah Restaurant noticed that every meal he ordered included radicchio. The waiter mentioned that they could make a risotto—not on the menu—that included radicchio! Thus was born the trademark Villa d'Este Risotto with Radicchio—straight from the diner's mouth to Luciano's ear!

Serves 4 to 6
One 7-ounce head radicchio
4 tablespoons butter
1 cup red wine
6 cups vegetable stock
1 small onion, finely chopped
2 cups Carnaroli rice
4½ ounces smoked Provolone cheese, cut into cubes
Salt and freshly ground black pepper to taste

1 Cut the radicchio in half and julienne one of the halves. Set aside. Slice the remaining half into lengthwise strips.

2 Melt 1 tablespoon of the butter in a medium sauté pan over medium heat. Add the radicchio strips and sauté for about 5 minutes, until softened. Pour the wine into the pan, let it evaporate, and continue cooking until tender, about 5 minutes.

3 Meanwhile, bring the stock to a boil in a medium saucepan, then reduce the heat and keep at a bare simmer.

4 Melt 1 tablespoon of the butter in a large, heavy saucepan over medium heat. Add the onion and cook, stirring constantly with a wooden spoon, until softened and translucent, about 3 minutes. Add the rice and cook, stirring, for about 3 minutes, until every grain is coated with butter.

5 Add 1 cup of the stock and stir until the liquid is absorbed. When the first cup of stock starts boiling, add the julienned (uncooked) radicchio. Continue adding stock, about ½ cup at a time, stirring frequently and making sure all the liquid is absorbed before adding more stock. Cook until the rice is just tender and creamy but still *al dente*, 15 to 20 minutes. You may have leftover stock.

6 Remove the pan from the heat and stir in the remaining 2 tablespoons butter, the Provolone cheese, and salt and pepper to taste. Let the risotto rest for a minute or two and serve on individual plates, decorated with the sautéed radicchio.

Raffaella Bruni, wife of the Mayor of Como, Luciano Parolari, and Jean-Marc Droulers of Villa d'Este.

Black Squid Ink Risotto
Risotto Nero di Seppie

Héctor Siracusano, a member of the Argentinean parliament, and his wife have been coming to Villa d'Este regularly for many years. The moment they are spotted in the dining room word spreads to the kitchen and, in a matter of minutes, the Siracusanos are served Black Squid Ink Risotto, their favorite dish. While many diners are put off by the idea of using black ink as a cooking ingredient, it takes only one taste before they, too, join the black squid ink club.

Serves 4 to 6
2½ pounds squid with ink sacs
4 tablespoons extra virgin olive oil
1 small onion, finely chopped
2 cloves garlic
1 cup dry white wine
2 tablespoons tomato sauce
6 cups fish stock
1 tablespoon butter
2 cups Carnaroli rice
1 tablespoon grated Parmesan cheese
3 tablespoons minced flat-leaf parsley
Salt and freshly ground black pepper to taste

1 Clean the squid, removing the ink sacs. Squeeze the ink from the sacs and set aside the liquid. Cut the squid into strips. Warm 2 tablespoons of the olive oil in a large sauté pan. Add half the onion, and garlic, and cook until lightly browned. Add the squid, the squid ink, wine and cook until the wine is reduced by half. Add the tomato sauce and cook for 30 minutes.

2 Meanwhile, prepare the risotto: Bring the stock to a boil in a medium saucepan, then reduce the heat and keep at a bare simmer.

3 Melt the butter in a large, heavy saucepan over medium heat. Add the remaining onion and cook, stirring constantly with a wooden spoon, until softened and translucent, about 3 minutes. Add the rice and cook, stirring, for about 3 minutes, until every grain is coated with butter.

4 Add 1 cup of the stock , the squid and their sauce and stir until the liquid is absorbed. Continue adding stock, about ½ cup at a time, stirring frequently and making sure all the liquid is absorbed before adding more stock. Cook until the rice is just tender and creamy but still *al dente*, 15 to 20 minutes. You may have leftover stock.

5 Remove the pan from the heat and stir in the remaining 2 tablespoons olive oil, the Parmesan cheese, parsley, and salt and pepper to taste. Let the risotto rest for a minute or two and serve piping hot and topped with the squid.

Fish Risottos

Risotto with Perch Fillets

Risotto con Pesce Persico

When Gianni Versace moved to Lake Como, he lived at Villa d'Este while his new favorite residence, Villa Le Fontanelle, located just around the bend from Villa d'Este on the lake, was being restored.

Risotto with fish was Gianni's preferred dish, and when he finally moved into his villa he often called on Luciano to be the chef for his dinner parties. Elton John was so enamored of Luciano's fare that he had his chef consigned to a fifteen-day apprenticeship to learn the secrets of Luciano's cooking.

Not only was this risotto a favorite of Gianni Versace, Madonna, and Elton John, but because of the inclusion of the daily catch, it makes it a specialty of Lake Como as well. If perch is not available, any fleshy fish of your choice will do.

Serves 6

6 cups chicken stock
2 tablespoons extra virgin olive oil
1 small onion, finely chopped
2 cups Carnaroli rice
½ cup dry white wine
5 tablespoons butter
24 small perch fillets, without skin,
    each weighing about 1/2 ounce
Salt and freshly ground black pepper to taste
A few sage leaves
½ lemon
3 tablespoons grated Parmesan cheese

1 Bring the stock to a boil in a medium saucepan, then reduce the heat and keep at a bare simmer.

2 Warm the olive oil in a large, heavy saucepan over medium heat. Add the onion and cook, stirring constantly with a wooden spoon, until softened and translucent, about 3 minutes. Add the rice and cook, stirring, for about 3 minutes, until every grain is coated with oil. Then add the wine and stir until absorbed.

3 Add 1 cup of the stock and stir until the liquid is absorbed. Continue adding stock, about ½ cup at a time, stirring frequently and making sure all the liquid is absorbed before adding more stock. Cook until the rice is just tender and creamy but still *al dente*, 15 to 20 minutes. You may have leftover stock.

4 While the risotto is cooking, warm 2 tablespoons of the butter in a large skillet over medium-high heat. Season the perch with salt and pepper. Add the perch to the skillet in batches, and cook until almost opaque, about 5 minutes. Turn the fish and cook for another minute, adding a few sage leaves and a sprinkle of lemon juice to the pan.

5 Remove the pan from the heat and stir in the remaining 3 tablespoons butter, the Parmesan cheese, and salt and pepper to taste. Let the risotto rest for a minute or two, then serve in individual plates with 4 perch fillets arranged around the risotto.

The Poster for the 1949 Italian film "Bitter Rice," starring Silvana Mangano, one of Italy's leading ladies, features Mangano in a rice (risotto) field and created nothing short of a sensation when it appeared in 1949.

Risotto with Seafood
Risotto ai Frutti di Mare

The American De Domenicos from Santa Fe, New Mexico, regulars at Villa d'Este, love Lake Como so much that they now have their own home on the lake. Inspired by Villa d'Este and the cuisine of Luciano, they write:

Our favorite recollection of risotto was when we tasted the fantastic Risotto with Seafood at The Grill Restaurant at Villa d'Este. I have to say, I think often about the expression of joy that crossed Maître d' Piazza's face as he put the dish before us: big chunks of fresh lobster and crisp, succulent scampi, all seasoned flawlessly in a risotto that was cooked to perfection. To this day I can still almost taste the deliciously rich flavors. Piazza let us know whenever The Grill's chef was serving this dish—and we ate gloriously well that summer. We have never had a risotto so good again.

Luciano's skills have humbled more than one experienced chef. Australian Noelene Keen Ward writes:

My husband, Rupert, was—or had the reputation for being, anyway—the best risotto maker in Sydney. That was until we visited Villa d'Este and experienced Luciano's risotto: This was very bad for Rupert's morale. Rupert attempted to relearn and modify his technique, as he wanted to be number one again, but he has now retired. He just can't do it! After all, he has no lake, only a harbor. And so he surrenders his crown, with pleasure. He can't wait to experience Luciano's Risotto with Seafood—his favorite, once more.

Serves 6
4 tablespoons extra virgin olive oil
2 cloves garlic, chopped
20 small clams
1 cup dry white wine
6 large shrimp, peeled and deveined
6 crayfish
6 scallops, cleaned
Salt and freshly ground black pepper to taste
3 cups fish stock and 3 cups chicken stock mixed together
1 small onion, thinly sliced

3 squid, cleaned and cut into rings
2 cups Carnaroli rice
3 tablespoons butter
Juice of ½ lemon
1 tablespoon chopped flat-leaf parsley
4 basil leaves, chopped

1 Warm 1 tablespoon of the olive oil in a large sauté pan over medium-high heat. Add half of the garlic, followed by the clams and ½ cup of the wine, and cook, covered, shaking the pan, until the clams open. Discard any clams that do not open. Reserve the liquid and set aside.

2 Warm 1 tablespoon of the olive oil in the sauté pan over medium heat, add the remaining garlic clove, the shrimp, crayfish, scallops, and salt and pepper to taste.

3 Bring the stock to a boil in a medium saucepan, then reduce the heat and keep at a bare simmer.

4 Warm the remaining 2 tablespoons olive oil in a large, heavy saucepan over medium heat. Add the onion and cook, stirring constantly with a wooden spoon, until softened and translucent, about 3 minutes. Add the squid and cook until lightly browned. Add the rice and cook, stirring, for about 3 minutes, until every grain is coated with oil. Then add the remaining ½ cup wine and stir until absorbed.

5 Add 1 cup of the stock and stir until the liquid is absorbed. Continue adding stock, about ½ cup at a time, stirring frequently and making sure all the liquid is absorbed before adding more stock. Cook until the rice is just tender and creamy but still *al dente*, 15 to 20 minutes. You may have leftover stock.

6 A couple of minutes before the rice is done add clams with their liquid and half of the fish .

7 Remove the pan from the heat and add the butter, lemon juice, parsley, basil, and salt and pepper to taste. Serve the risotto on individual plates, garnished with the remaining shrimp, crayfish, and scallops.

Risotto with Stuffed Cuttlefish and Basil

Risotto con Seppioline Farcite e Basilico

When the Duke and Duchess of Windsor visited Villa d'Este for the first time (the first of many visits they would make to Villa d'Este), they were still Wallis Simpson and Edward, Prince of Wales. The first photograph ever taken of them together, in fact, was shot at Villa d'Este as they embarked on the hotel launch. Every time the Duchess would board the launch on subsequent visits, she would declare, "Same lake, same moon, and same boat—how romantic!"

One of the other memorable aspects of their visits was their affection for this esoteric risotto with cuttlefish and basil. Always adventurous eaters, they found the dish both hearty and elegant, and no matter what else they ordered during their stay, the kitchen knew they would begin their visit to the hotel with this risotto.

Serves 6

2 slices white bread, crusts removed and cubed
2 tablespoons milk
2 ounces cooked spinach, coarsely chopped
1 large egg
2 tablespoons grated pecorino cheese
½ clove garlic, minced
2 tomatoes, peeled and seeded, cut into small cubes
Salt and freshly ground black pepper to taste
3 tablespoons extra virgin olive oil
24 small cuttlefish, cleaned (6 cut into small strips)
2 onions, 1 thinly sliced and 1 finely chopped
2 cups dry white wine
4 cups vegetable stock and 3 cups fish stock, mixed together
4 tablespoons butter
2 cups Carnaroli rice
3 tablespoons grated Parmesan cheese
1 tablespoon minced basil, plus basil leaves for garnish

1 In a large bowl, combine the bread with the milk. Let it rest until the bread becomes soft, about 5 minutes, mixing with a fork. Then add the spinach, egg, pecorino cheese, garlic, half the tomatoes, salt and pepper to taste, and 1 tablespoon of the olive oil. Mix well and stuff the cuttlefish with the mixture, then close each of them with a toothpick.

2 Warm 1 tablespoon of the olive oil in a large, heavy saucepan over medium heat, add the thinly sliced onion, and sauté for about 3 minutes, until softened. Add the cuttlefish and the remaining tomatoes, and cook for 3 minutes. Add 1 cup of the wine, let evaporate, then add 1 cup of the stock. Cover, reduce the heat to low, and cook for 20 to 30 minutes, until the cuttlefish is cooked through.

3 Meanwhile, prepare the risotto: Bring the remaining stock to a boil in a medium saucepan, then reduce the heat and keep at a bare simmer.

4 Melt 1 tablespoon of the butter with the remaining 1 tablespoon olive oil in a large, heavy saucepan over medium heat. Add the finely chopped onion and cook, stirring constantly with a wooden spoon, until softened and translucent, about 3 minutes. Add the rice and cook, stirring, for about 3 minutes, until every grain is coated with butter and oil. Then add the remaining 1 cup wine and stir until absorbed.

5 Add 1 cup of the stock and stir until the liquid is absorbed. Continue adding stock, about ½ cup at a time, stirring frequently and making sure all the liquid is absorbed before adding more stock. Halfway through cooking the risotto, add the reserved cuttlefish strips. Continue adding stock. Cook until the rice is just tender and creamy but still *al dente*, 15 to 20 minutes. You may have leftover stock.

6 Remove the pan from the heat and stir in the remaining 3 tablespoons butter, the Parmesan cheese, minced basil, and salt and pepper to taste. Let the risotto rest for a minute or two and serve on individual dishes, topped with the cuttlefish and garnished with fresh basil leaves.

Risotto with Smoked Salmon
Risotto al Salmone Affumicato

This risotto is associated with some of the most famous people to have visited Villa d'Este—or certainly those who have the biggest reputations. For example, in the December 1972 issue of *Gourmet* magazine, James Beard wrote a story about rice, which was quite important because most people, especially Americans, at the time had no idea what risotto or Italian cooked rice was. He prominently featured this Risotto with Smoked Salmon recipe and named it *Risotto Villa d'Este*, having first tasted it on a visit to the hotel. To this day, hotel guests refer to the dish as James Beard's Risotto.

Bill Wright tells a story about Luciano Pavarotti and the famous James Beard's Risotto:

When I was working with Pavarotti, he was on a boiled rice diet until he insisted on cooking it himself, at which point he turned the dish into a non-dietetic, deluxe version with smoked salmon. Then he would sit on a high stool, his back to the stove, and stir, stir, stir while looking at me and talking about his life. He hated doing this (talking about his life), but thanks to the risotto and the length of time it took to make it perfectly, I got lots of good information from him both about his life and how to make the perfect James Beard's Risotto.

Serves 4 to 6
1 tablespoon extra virgin olive oil
1 cup diced or shredded smoked salmon
⅓ cup Scotch whiskey
6 cups chicken stock
3 tablespoons butter
1 small onion, finely chopped
2 cups Carnaroli rice
1 tablespoon grated Parmesan cheese
Lemon juice to taste
Salt and freshly ground black pepper to taste
Caviar, for serving (optional)

1 Warm the olive oil in a medium sauté pan over medium heat. Add the salmon and sauté for 3 minutes. Pour the Scotch over the salmon and let it practically evaporate. Then cook, without boiling, for 1 minute, remove from the heat, and set aside.

2 Meanwhile, bring the stock to a boil in a medium saucepan, then reduce the heat and keep at a bare simmer.

3 Melt 1 tablespoon of the butter in a large, heavy saucepan over medium heat. Add the onion and cook, stirring constantly with a wooden spoon, until softened and translucent, about 3 minutes. Add the rice and cook, stirring, for about 3 minutes, until every grain is coated with butter.

4 Add 1 cup of the stock and stir until the liquid is absorbed. Continue adding stock, about ½ cup at a time, stirring frequently and making sure all the liquid is absorbed before adding more stock. Cook until the rice is just tender and creamy but still *al dente*, 15 to 20 minutes. You may have leftover stock.

5 Remove the pan from the heat and stir in the remaining 2 tablespoons butter, the Parmesan cheese, and lemon juice and salt and pepper to taste.

6 If you really want to splurge, a dollop of caviar over the risotto and a few drops of lemon juice will turn this into a most elegant dish for a special dinner party. It can also be served as a main course, according to fashion designer Lorenzo Riva, who spends most of his weekends at Villa d'Este entertaining friends.

Risotto with Lemon and Shrimp
Risotto al Limone con Scampi

Olympic gold medal ice-skating champion Kristi Yamaguchi and her husband, Brett Hedican, star defenseman for the North Carolina Hurricane hockey team, spent their honeymoon at Villa d'Este during the summer of 2000, and they often indulged in our risottos. When I ran into them in Raleigh-Durham, where Brett was playing, I asked which risotto he and Kristi preferred. Brett replied immediately: "Kristi and I loved the seafood risottos, especially the one with shrimp." If their cooking skills are as good as their fancy footwork, Kristi and Brett can now indulge in this Villa d'Este classic whenever they get the craving.

Ian and Judith Forbes have been spending their summers on the shores of Lake Como and the Villa d'Este for over thirty-years, and admit to hardly leaving the premises because they like to have all their meals in the hotel. When the maître d' lets them know that Risotto with Lemon and Shrimp is on the Verandah menu, they make a point of eating there.

Serves 4 to 6

Shrimp Sauce
2 tablespoons extra virgin olive oil
24 large shrimp, peeled and deveined
1 cup dry white wine

Risotto
6 cups fish stock
5 tablespoons butter
1 tablespoon finely chopped shallot or spring onion
2 cups Carnaroli rice
2 tablespoons grated Parmesan cheese
1 tablespoon minced flat-leaf parsley
Juice of ½ lemon
Grated rind of ½ lemon
Salt and freshly ground black pepper to taste

Caramelized Lemon Rind
Julienned rind of 1 lemon
1 cup white wine
2 tablespoons sugar

1 To make the shrimp sauce, warm the olive oil in a large sauté pan over medium-high heat. Add the shrimp and cook for about 5 minutes, until the shrimp are pink and firm. Add the wine and stir until the liquid is absorbed.

2 Meanwhile, bring the stock to a boil in a medium saucepan, then reduce the heat and keep at a bare simmer.

3 Melt 2 tablespoons of the butter in a large, heavy saucepan over medium heat. Add the shallot and cook, stirring constantly with a wooden spoon, until softened and translucent, about 3 minutes. Add the rice and cook, stirring, for about 3 minutes, until every grain is coated with butter.

4 Add 1 cup of the stock and stir until the liquid is absorbed. Continue adding stock, about ½ cup at a time, stirring frequently and making sure all the liquid is absorbed before adding more stock. Halfway through cooking the risotto, add half the shrimp and their sauce. Reserve the

Shellfish Risottos

remaining shrimp as a garnish. Continue adding the stock. Cook until the rice is just tender and creamy but still *al dente*, 15 to 20 minutes. You may have leftover stock.

5 While the risotto is cooking, make the caramelized lemon rind: Place the julienned lemon rind in a pot of boiling water for a few minutes, then drain and pat dry with paper towels. Warm the wine and sugar in a saucepan over medium heat. Add the lemon rind and cook, stirring, until caramelized, about 10 minutes.

6 When the risotto is done, remove the pan from the heat and stir in the remaining 3 tablespoons butter, the Parmesan cheese, parsley, lemon juice, grated lemon rind, and salt and pepper to taste. Let the risotto rest for a minute or two and serve, topped with the remaining shrimp and the caramelized lemon rind.

Risotto with Lobster and Crayfish
Risotto con Aragosta e Gamberi

Risotto is a fine addition to any fairy tale wedding reception, like the reception my godchild, Samantha Slaney, had when she got married at the Villa d'Este. The Lucullan dinner, consisting of many delicious dishes, featured a fabulous Risotto with Lobster and Crayfish, lovingly prepared by Luciano. This is a recipe to share with anyone about to say their vows; the combination of Lobster and Crayfish is the perfect way to express true love.

Serves 6
One 1-pound lobster
2 tablespoons extra virgin olive oil
2 shallots, thinly sliced
1 bay leaf
2 ounces cherry tomatoes
¼ cup Cognac
1 cup dry white wine
1 cup chicken stock
1 clove garlic, chopped
12 crayfish

5 cups fish stock
2 tablespoons butter
1 small onion, finely chopped
2 cups Carnaroli rice
2 tablespoons grated Parmesan cheese
1 tablespoon minced flat-leaf parsley
Juice of ½ lemon
Salt and freshly ground black pepper to taste

1 Cut the lobster in half lengthwise. Warm 1 tablespoon of the olive oil in a large sauté pan over medium-high heat. Add the lobster and cook for 2 minutes.

2 Add the shallots, bay leaf, and cherry tomatoes and cook for 5 minutes, then flambé with the Cognac and wine. When evaporated, add the chicken stock and cook for 10 to 15 minutes, until the lobster meat is cooked through. Let cool slightly, then remove the meat from the lobster carcass, saving the head for garnish.

3 In a separate sauté pan, warm the remaining 1 tablespoon olive oil over medium heat. Add the garlic and crayfish and cook for 2 minutes.

4 Meanwhile, make the risotto: bring the fish stock to a boil in a medium saucepan, then reduce the heat and keep at a bare simmer.

5 Melt 1 tablespoon of the butter in a large, heavy saucepan over medium heat. Add the onion and cook, stirring constantly with a wooden spoon, until softened and translucent, about 3 minutes. Add the rice and cook, stirring, for about 3 minutes, until every grain is coated with butter.

6 Add 1 cup of the stock and stir until the liquid is absorbed. Continue adding stock, about ½ cup at a time, stirring frequently and making sure all the liquid is absorbed before adding more stock. After you finish adding the stock, add the lobster cooking sauce. Cook until the rice is just tender and creamy but still *al dente*, 15 to 20 minutes. You may have leftover stock. Remove the pan from the heat and stir in the remaining 1 tablespoon butter, the Parmesan cheese, parsley, lemon juice, and salt and pepper to taste. Let the risotto rest for a minute or two and serve on individual plates, garnished with the lobster meat, lobster head, and the crayfish.

Risotto Mantecato with Clams, Zucchini Blossoms, and Wild Asparagus

*Risotto Mantecato con Vongole Veraci,
Fior di Zucchine, Asparagi Selvatici*

As the head chef of Villa d'Este, Luciano has developed more than a few fail-safe personal favorites, and this recipe is one of them. The reason why it's among Luciano's favorite is simple: the salty flavor of the clams combined with the dramatic appearance of the fried zucchini blossoms and the crisp crunch of wild asparagus transforms this smooth and creamy risotto into a flavor sensation. The texture is at once complex yet subtle and, as always, perfectly delectable.

Serves 4 to 6
3 tablespoons extra virgin olive oil
1 clove garlic
2 cups small clams in their shells
6 cups fish stock
2 small shallots, minced
2 cups Carnaroli rice
1 cup dry white wine
12 zucchini blossoms
Salt and freshly ground black pepper to taste
1 small bunch wild asparagus, parboiled
Parmesan cheese, for serving

1 Warm 1 tablespoon of the olive oil in a large sauté pan over medium-high heat. Add the garlic and clams, ½ cup dry white wine, cover, and cook, shaking the pan, until the shells open. Discard any clams that don't open. Discard the shells and return the clams to their liquid. Set aside.

2 Bring the stock to a boil in a medium saucepan, then reduce the heat and keep at a bare simmer.

3 Warm 1 tablespoon of the olive oil in a large, heavy saucepan over medium heat. Add the shallots and cook, stirring constantly with a wooden spoon, until softened and translucent, about 3 minutes. Add the rice and cook, stirring, for about 3 minutes, until every grain is coated with oil. Then add the remaining wine and stir until absorbed.

4 Add 1 cup of the stock and stir until the liquid is absorbed. Continue adding stock, about ½ cup at a time, stirring frequently and making sure all the liquid is absorbed before adding more stock. Cook until the rice is just tender and creamy but still *al dente*, 15 to 20 minutes. You may have leftover stock.

5 While the risotto is cooking, warm the remaining 1 tablespoon olive oil in a medium sauté pan over medium heat. Add the zucchini blossoms and cook for about 3 minutes, until softened.

6 When the risotto is finished, remove the pan from the heat and add the clams with their liquid and salt and pepper to taste. Mix well. Let the risotto rest for a minute or two and serve on individual plates, decorated with the zucchini blossoms and asparagus and sprinkled with Parmesan cheese.

Risotto with Prosecco Sparkling Wine and Oysters
Risotto con Prosecco e Ostriche

Donald and Ann Petroni visited Villa d'Este on their honeymoon in 1973. Don, who is a true gourmet, spent a lot of time in the kitchens of Villa d'Este, so he was able to perfect his skills in cooking risotto and make a *bella figura* among his friends upon returning home. We consider this recipe a bella figura risotto to complement Donald's cooking skills.

Serves 6

30 oysters (preferably Belon or Creuse from Portugal)

2 cups Prosecco

3 tablespoons butter

6 cups vegetable stock

1 tablespoon extra virgin olive oil

1 small onion, finely chopped

2 cups Carnaroli rice

3 tablespoons grated Parmesan cheese

Salt and freshly ground black pepper to taste

1 teaspoon chopped chives

1 Shuck the oysters and place them with their water in a medium saucepan over medium-high heat. Add 1 cup of the Prosecco, bring to a boil, and cook for 45 seconds. Remove the oysters, and cook to reduce the liquid. Then add 1 tablespoon of the butter and mix well to obtain a creamy consistency.

2 Meanwhile, prepare the risotto: Bring the stock to a boil in a medium saucepan, then reduce the heat and keep at a bare simmer.

3 Melt 1 tablespoon of the butter with the olive oil in a large, heavy saucepan over medium heat. Add the onion and cook, stirring constantly with a wooden spoon, until softened and translucent, about 3 minutes. Add the rice and cook, stirring, for about 3 minutes, until every grain is coated with butter and oil. Then add ½ cup of the Prosecco and stir until absorbed.

4 Add 1 cup of the stock and stir until the liquid is absorbed. Continue adding stock, about ½ cup at a time, stirring frequently and making sure all the liquid is absorbed before adding more stock. Cook until the rice is just tender and creamy but still *al dente*, 15 to 20 minutes. You may have leftover stock.

5 Remove the pan from the heat and stir in the oysters, remaining 1 tablespoon butter, the Parmesan cheese, salt and pepper to taste, and the remaining half cup Prosecco. Let the risotto rest for a minute or two and serve on individual plates decorated with the chives.

Risotto with Scallops Flavored with Rosemary

Risotto con Noci di Capesante al Rosmarino

While several people truly love to indulge in eating risotto, one of my dearest friends, Harriette Delsener, is not one of them. She never eats risotto! To sway her taste buds (and if you, too, have any friends who are also missing out on the joys of risotto), we offer this delicious recipe.

Serves 6

24 scallops, cleaned
Salt and freshly ground black pepper to taste
4 tablespoons extra virgin olive oil
1 shallot, finely chopped
2 cups dry white wine
6 cups fish stock
1 tablespoon butter
1 small onion, finely chopped
2 cups Carnaroli rice
1 teaspoon minced fresh rosemary
  mixed with 2 tablespoons butter
3 tablespoons grated Parmesan cheese
Rosemary sprigs, for garnish

1 Cut 6 of the scallops into cubes, season with salt and pepper to taste, and set aside.

2 Warm 1 tablespoon of the olive oil in a large sauté pan over medium-high heat. Add the shallots and sauté for 3 minutes. Add the whole scallops and cook for about 2 minutes per side, until lightly browned and almost cooked through. Add salt and pepper to taste and 1 cup of the wine. Cook, stirring, until the wine is absorbed. Set aside for garnish.

3 Bring the stock to a boil in a medium saucepan, then reduce the heat and keep at a bare simmer.

4 Melt the butter in a large, heavy saucepan over medium heat. Add the onion and cook, stirring constantly with a wooden spoon, until softened and translucent, about 3 minutes. Add the rice and cook, stirring, for about 3 minutes, until every grain is coated with butter. Then add the remaining 1 cup wine and stir until absorbed.

5 Add 1 cup of the stock and stir until the liquid is absorbed. Continue adding stock, about ½ cup at a time, stirring frequently and making sure all the liquid is absorbed before adding more stock. Cook until the rice is just tender and creamy but still *al dente*, 15 to 20 minutes. You may have leftover stock.

6 Add the cubed scallops to the risotto. Remove the pan from the heat and stir in the rosemary-butter mixture, the remaining 3 tablespoons olive oil, the Parmesan cheese, and salt and pepper to taste. Let the risotto rest for a minute or two and serve on individual dishes garnished with the whole scallops and rosemary sprigs.

Risotto and Shrimp Carthusian
Risotto alla Certosina

In the 1970s, Julie Dannenbaum decided to start Philadelphia's Creative Cooking School and was invited to give cooking classes at the Gritti Palace Hotel in Venice. When she heard that we had started to offer cooking classes at Villa d'Este, she dropped by to see us. Impressed by Luciano's cuisine, Julie invited him to appear as a guest chef at her school. She once remarked that she liked all risotto as long as Luciano was in the kitchen. When pressed to reveal a favorite, she answered, "One dish Luciano introduced me to is the risotto with shrimp and green peas, which I still make when I'm hosting a dinner party!"

And so we share with you this delectable and unforgettable party pleaser.

Serves 4 to 6
6 cups fish or chicken stock
3 tablespoons extra virgin olive oil
2 small onions, finely chopped

2 cups shrimp

½ cup brandy

1 cup green peas, cooked

6 tablespoons tomato sauce

Salt and freshly ground black pepper to taste

4 tablespoons butter

2 cups Carnaroli rice

1 tablespoon grated Parmesan cheese

1 Bring the stock to a boil in a medium saucepan, then reduce the heat and keep at a bare simmer.

2 Warm 1 tablespoon of the olive oil in a large, heavy saucepan over medium heat. Add half of the chopped onion and cook, stirring constantly with a wooden spoon, until softened and translucent, about 3 minutes. Add the shrimp and brandy. When half of the brandy has been absorbed, add the green peas and tomato sauce and stir until cooked through. Season with salt and pepper to taste and set aside.

3 Melt 1 tablespoon of the butter with 1 tablespoon of the olive oil in another large, heavy saucepan over medium heat. Add the remaining chopped onion and cook, stirring constantly with a wooden spoon, until softened and translucent, about 3 minutes. Add the rice and cook, stirring, for about 3 minutes, until every grain is coated with butter and oil.

4 Add 1 cup of the stock and stir until the liquid is absorbed. Continue adding stock, about ½ cup at a time, stirring frequently and making sure all the liquid is absorbed before adding more stock. After 10 minutes, add half of the shrimp and pea mixture. Continue adding stock. Cook until the rice is just tender and creamy but still *al dente*, 15 to 20 minutes. You may have leftover stock.

5 Remove the pan from the heat and stir in the remaining shrimp and pea mixture, remaining 3 tablespoons butter, remaining 1 tablespoon olive oil, the Parmesan cheese, and salt and pepper to taste. Let the risotto rest for a minute or two and serve piping hot.

The fortresses from which you can enjoy an enchanting view of the lake, were a Christmas gift of Countess Vittoria to her husband Domenico Pino, a Napoleonic General. The General was so delighted with the idea that he recruited a group of military cadets to play mock battles here.

Autumn

Risotto with Pumpkin Blossoms and White Truffles
Risotto con Fiori di Zucca e Tartufo Bianco

Event planner Elizabeth Rich from Sydney provides one the best testimonials for Luciano's risotto. She first visited Villa d'Este about eighteen years ago, and by chance she arrived in September as the truffle season was starting. Since 1986, Elizabeth has visited every September to enjoy this dish. So beloved is this dish, in fact, that Luciano prepared it at the James Beard House on November 18, 2002, to celebrate his Silver Jubilee as Executive Chef at Villa d'Este. And as if that weren't enough, it was this very recipe that inspired us to compile a book of all of the wonderful risottos that Luciano has made famous.

Risotto and truffles make for a delectable combination; its fans include magazine editor Pamela Fiori, publicist David Carriere, and countless members of Italian royalty. David remembers:

" When I was there in December 1999, the hotel was in a flurry of activities and people as the eve of the millennium was approaching. To mark the occasion, the kitchen prepared a special truffle-themed dinner which Jean Salvadore asked me to attend. Just as the risotto arrived at the table, so did a countess, who proceeded to say hello to Jean. They shared a brief, pleasant exchange, introductions were made, and after the countess departed, I announced with some excitement that I had never met an authentic countess before. Jean quickly replied, "My dear, don't get too excited. There are more countesses around here than there are truffles for your risotto." "

Risotto with *Black* Truffle, which was photographed when white truffles were out-of-season.

Seasonal Risottos

Serves 4 to 6
7 cups chicken stock
50 pumpkin blossoms
3 tablespoons butter
Sea salt to taste
2 tablespoons extra virgin olive oil
1 small onion, finely chopped
2 cups Carnaroli rice
½ cup dry white wine
3 tablespoon grated Parmesan cheese
1 small white truffle (about 1 ounce), for shaving

1 Bring the stock to a boil in a medium saucepan, then reduce the heat
and keep at a bare simmer.

2 Separate the pumpkin blossom petals from the stems; wash and dry
thoroughly and cut into 4 pieces each. Warm 2 tablespoons of the butter
in a medium saucepan over medium heat. Add the pumpkin blossoms and
cook for 1 minute. Add 1 cup stock, and cook for 10 to 15 minutes. Add
salt to taste and remove from the heat.

3 Melt the remaining 1 tablespoon butter with the olive oil in a large, heavy
saucepan over medium heat. Add the onion and cook, stirring constantly
with a wooden spoon, until softened and translucent, about 3 minutes. Add
the rice and cook, stirring, for about 3 minutes, until every grain is coated
with butter and oil. Then add the wine and stir until absorbed.

4 Add 1 cup of the stock and stir until the liquid is absorbed. Continue
adding stock, about ½ cup at a time, stirring frequently and making sure
all the liquid is absorbed before adding more stock. After 10 to 12 minutes,
add the pumpkin blossoms and stir well. Continue to add stock. Cook until
the rice is just tender and creamy but still *al dente*, 15 to 20 minutes. You
may have leftover stock.

5 Remove the pan from the heat and stir in the Parmesan cheese and salt to
taste. Let the risotto rest for a minute or two and serve on individual plates,
topped with a shaving of truffle.

All About the Truffle

You are planning to host a dinner party at home and want to make *bella figura* and money is no object.

How about a risotto with white truffles?

White truffles are found in the Piedmont region of northern Italy in the woods outside the medieval town of Alba on the roots of oak trees, willows, hazelnut trees, and poplars. The truffles are unearthed by dogs who have been trained for this precise purpose.

The season starts in September and lasts until November, and truffles can turn quickly. Only a few stores carry this exclusive and expensive ingredient, so make sure any tuber you purchase is packaged correctly and there is an absence of mold.

To preserve your truffles you can place them in a glass jar filled with uncooked rice or wrap them in newspaper and place in the refrigerator. Preservation is the best way to protect your truffles, as once they are unearthed they last for only about a week. It is important to examine your truffles frequently. Any suspicious truffle should be discarded.

Winter

Milanese Risotto with Saffron
Risotto alla Milanese

It takes a good deal of practice to make a good risotto, but once the techniques have been mastered, every chef can create his or her own signature dish—because there is no end to what can be added to risotto to give it a special twist. According to legend, in 1574 a painter working on the construction of the Milan Duomo dropped some saffron—in those days used only to mix colors—into his risotto lunch, creating what is now the quintessential and classic risotto. Whether he did this intentionally or by mistake (which seems more likely), I think it is a shame that this mouthwatering dish is not named after him!

During the 1960s and early 1970s, Alfred Hitchcock and his wife, Alma, would spend a fortnight at Villa d'Este in the month of September. It was their annual holiday, and they always looked forward to it. They never left the premises, and we had to make sure that there would be no paparazzi in sight—otherwise they would pack up and leave.

Only once did some photographers show up, at the cocktail hour. Hitchcock was about to throw a tantrum, but he calmed down when he was told that the photographers had been hired to cover an important wedding taking place at Villa d'Este—even if he was recognized they would ignore him. I wonder to this day whether the great movie director wasn't a bit disappointed that the photographers were not there to see him.

Hitchcock was quite a gourmet, and he had a passion for risottos, which in his day were for the most part only available in Italy, and primarily in northern Italy. Mario Arrigo, who at the time was the general manager of the hotel, would accompany Hitchcock to the kitchen every day to confer with Luciano while Hitchcock chose his meal. He tasted every kind of risotto, and it became a challenge for Luciano to keep creating new versions, from Risotto with White Truffles to Milanese Risotto with Ossobuco. At the end of one of his stays, Hitchcock gave us permission to organize a press conference in the kitchen. What a turnout! Italian television shot a movie, with Hitchcock as the main actor. He donned the chef's toque and chased all the kitchen staff around with a big carving knife.

Serves 4

6 cups chicken stock

1 tablespoon extra virgin olive oil

1 small onion, finely chopped

2 ox beef marrow (optional)

2 cups Carnaroli rice

¼ teaspoon saffron threads

2 tablespoons butter

6 tablespoons grated Parmesan cheese,
  plus more for serving

Salt and freshly ground black pepper to taste

1 Bring the stock to a boil in a medium saucepan, then reduce the heat and keep at a bare simmer.

2 Warm the olive oil in a large, heavy saucepan over medium heat. Add the onion and beef marrow, if using, and cook, stirring constantly with a wooden spoon, until softened and translucent, about 3 minutes. Add the rice and cook, stirring, for about 3 minutes, until every grain is coated with oil.

3 Add 1 cup of the stock and stir until the liquid is absorbed. Continue adding stock, about ½ cup at a time, stirring frequently and making sure all the liquid is absorbed before adding more stock. When half the stock has been added, add the saffron. Continue to add stock. Cook until the rice is just tender and creamy but still *al dente*, 15 to 20 minutes. You may have leftover stock.

4 Remove the pan from the heat and stir in the butter, Parmesan cheese, and salt and pepper to taste.

5 Let the risotto rest for 2 to 3 minutes to absorb the full color of the saffron—it should have a strong yellow color. Serve on individual plates with additional Parmesan cheese on the side.

Ossobuco Milanese

Ossobuco alla Milanese

One of the great things about Milanese Risotto is that it has a perfect meat accompaniment: ossobuco. Hotel guest Margaret Beery explains how risotto and ossobuco are married in the minds of many:

" In my part of the world, Tex-Mex food and chicken fried steak are king, explaining why in 1999 risotto was entirely foreign to me, as was ossobuco. On my first night at Villa d'Este, my romance with risotto—usually accompanied by ossobuco—began.

My heaven-sent month by Lake Como gave me a chance to relish every inventive risotto Chef Luciano prepared. During my first stay at the hotel, I struck up a friendship with Jean Salvadore, who arranged a trip to the kitchen to see the risotti in progress (although I must admit my eyes did wander to the prepping of numerous gelati, as well!).

On my final evening at the Villa, lovely flowers graced the table, champagne chilled in a silver bucket—all that was missing from the perfectly laid table was a menu. And there was to be none, I soon discovered. As if by magic, Luciano appeared at the table: "Madame," he said, "for your last dinner at the Villa we've prepared all of your favorites."

Voilà. From the kitchen came a sampling of every risotto I'd exclaimed over, a fanfare of many items I loved, right down to the tasty morsels of the accompanying ossobuco and at least ten desserts. I can imagine nowhere but Villa d'Este where this kind of excitement would accompany a meal of such perfection. "

Ossobuco Milanese.

Serves 8
6 cups chicken stock, plus more if needed
All-purpose flour, to coat the shanks
Salt and freshly ground black pepper to taste
8 veal shinbones with marrow (about 2 inches long each)
2 tablespoons butter
2 tablespoons extra virgin olive oil
1 tablespoon finely chopped carrot
1 tablespoon finely chopped onion
1 tablespoon finely chopped celery
1 cup dry white wine
2 to 3 tablespoons Tomato Sauce (recipe follows)
   or 1 fresh tomato, coarsely chopped

Gremolada
3 tablespoons chopped flat-leaf parsley
1 large clove garlic, crushed
Grated rind of 1 lemon

1 Bring the stock to a boil in a medium saucepan, then reduce the heat and keep at a bare simmer.

2 Season the flour with salt and pepper to taste and coat the veal with the flour. Heat the butter and oil in a large saucepan over medium-high heat. Add the veal and brown on all sides. Remove the meat from the pan and add the carrot, onion, and celery to the pan. Sauté for about 5 minutes, until the vegetables have softened. Add the wine and reduce slightly. Return the meat to the saucepan. Add the tomato sauce and cover with stock, adding 1 cup at a time as needed. Cover and cook gently until tender. Cooking time varies according to the quality of the meat, but will be about 1 ½ to 2 hours. If the sauce is too thin, remove the meat from the pan, raise the heat, and reduce the sauce further.

3 While the veal is cooking, make the Gremolada by combining the parsley, garlic, and lemon rind.

3 Just before serving, sprinkle the Gremolada over the meat.

TOMATO SAUCE

2 pounds fresh ripe Italian plum tomatoes
    or one 28-ounce can peeled plum tomatoes
4 tablespoons extra virgin olive oil
1 small red onion, coarsely chopped
1 bay leaf
Salt and freshly ground black pepper to taste
Pinch of sugar (optional)
2 or 3 fresh basil leaves
1 garlic clove, finely chopped

1 Chop the tomatoes in a blender or by hand. Warm the olive oil in a medium saucepan over medium heat. Add the onion and the garlic and sauté until golden, about 5 minutes. Add the tomatoes and bay leaf. Season lightly with salt and pepper. Taste and if you find the sauce a little bitter, add the sugar. Simmer, stirring occasionally with a wooden spoon, for about 30 minutes, until the sauce has thickened. Add the basil and remove the bay leaf. Let cool and refrigerate any sauce you're not using immediately.

A view of Lake Como from the hills of the kitchen garden, where Luciano picks fresh basil for his tomato sauce.

Spring

Risotto with Spring Vegetables
Risotto Primavera

This risotto is a favorite of visitors to the hotel for two reasons: 1) since it's studded with vegetables rather than more fattening ingredients, diners can pretend that it's low in fat; and 2) the velvety texture and taste of the risotto base are perfectly counterbalanced by the crunchy texture of the fresh vegetables.

This risotto happens to be a favorite of Luciano himself and one that he earmarks as his most memorable in the thirty-eight years that he has been in the kitchen of Villa d'Este. Without hesitation, he commented: "In 1996, I made a risotto for Pope John Paul II. He came to Como for three days and was the guest of the archbishop, who called Villa d'Este and asked for our chef to prepare his meals. I made up a menu consisting of light chicken broth, steamed vegetables, and stewed fruit. His Holiness sent word back that he wanted a risotto with vegetables! Before his return to Rome, he thanked me in person and we were photographed together."

Even if you don't have the Pope over for dinner, this recipe is sure to be a memorable one, no matter with whom you share it.

Visitor Abby Levy writes that when she travelled to Italy for cooking classes in the Villa d'Este kitchen, she learned from the master himself how to fashion this perfect risotto, which is her favorite. She learned from Luciano to use only the freshest and best ingredients, keep it simple, and not be afraid to be creative. She also learned from Luciano to enjoy cooking more than ever before because he taught her to believe in her own kitchen competence.

Luciano greets Pope John Paul XXIII.

Harlene Horowitz tells a funny story about how she and her husband, Bob, first attempted to recreate this risotto after they had discovered it at Villa d'Este:

Last month Bob and I decided to cook a risotto. Because risotto can turn out to be a mass of rice stuck together like a blob, we decided to make two batches. Our first batch was so heavy it didn't even remotely resemble risotto; in fact, it wouldn't even go down the drain. We quickly discovered that the secret to making risotto is constant stirring. So for the second batch I was a vigilant stirrer and mixed the ingredients, finally, to a successful finish. Because we're health-conscious Californians, we added seasonal fresh vegetables to our second batch. Granted, it wasn't on par with Villa d'Este's menu, but for us it was certainly better than our first attempt and tasted utterly delicious.

Serves 6

6 cups vegetable stock
2 tablespoons extra virgin olive oil
1 small onion, chopped
2 cups Carnaroli rice
½ cup dry white wine
1 carrot, diced
1 celery stalk, chopped
½ red pepper, chopped (optional)
1/2 yellow pepper, chopped (optional)
3 ½ ounces string beans, trimmed and chopped
1 zucchini, diced
½ cup fresh green peas
3 ounces Taleggio cheese, diced
2 tablespoons butter
2 tablespoons grated Parmesan cheese, plus more for serving
2 tablespoons minced flat-leaf parsley
6 basil leaves, minced
Salt and freshly ground black pepper to taste

Risotto with Spring Vegetables.

1 Bring the stock to a boil in a medium saucepan, then reduce the heat and keep at a bare simmer.

2 Heat the olive oil in a large, heavy saucepan over medium heat. Add the onion and cook, stirring constantly with a wooden spoon, until softened and translucent, about 3 minutes. Add the rice and cook, stirring, for about 3 minutes, until every grain is coated with oil. Then add the wine and stir until absorbed.

3 Add 1 cup of the stock and stir until the liquid is absorbed. When the stock comes to a boil, add the carrot, celery, bell pepper, string beans, zucchini, and peas. Continue adding stock, about ½ cup at a time, stirring frequently and making sure all the liquid is absorbed before adding more stock. Continue to add stock. Cook until the rice is just tender and creamy but still *al dente*, 15 to 20 minutes. You may have leftover stock.

4 Remove the pan from the heat and stir in the Taleggio cheese, butter, Parmesan cheese, parsley, basil, and salt and pepper to taste. Let the risotto rest for a minute or two and serve with additional Parmesan cheese on the side.

Summer

Risotto with Green Tomatoes, Crispy Bacon, and Fava Beans

Risotto con i Pomodori Verdi, la Pancetta Affumicata Croccante e le Fave

Sandy Olin, a lovely lady from Asheville, North Carolina, learned the secrets to Luciano's trade when she attended several of his cooking classes. She writes:

My sister and I had prepared a barbecue reception and included Risotto with Green Tomatoes and Crispy Bacon, a recipe I learned while studying at Villa d'Este. For the next few days, we had the pleasure of eating risotto for breakfast, lunch, and dinner; there was so much left over.

Serves 4 to 6
6 cups vegetable stock
5½ ounces bacon (cut into 6 strips
   and cube the remaining meat)
1 shallot, thinly sliced
7 ounces green cherry tomatoes, blanched,
   peeled, and cut into cubes
2 cups Carnaroli rice
1 cup dry white wine
10 ounces fava beans, cooked in salted water,
drained, cooled, and peeled
3 tablespoons butter
3 tablespoons grated Parmesan cheese
Salt and freshly ground black pepper to taste

1 Bring the stock to a boil in a medium saucepan, then reduce the heat and keep at a bare simmer.

2 In a large, heavy saucepan, cook the bacon strips until crisp. Remove from the pan and drain on paper towels. Set aside. Add the cubed bacon to the pan and cook until well done. Discard most of the bacon grease, add the shallot and tomatoes and cook for 5 minutes. Leave the shallot, bacon, and tomatoes in the pan and, using the same pan, start making the risotto.

3 Add the rice and cook, stirring, for about 3 minutes, until every grain is coated with butter and oil. Then add the wine and stir until absorbed.

4 Add 1 cup of the stock and stir until the liquid is absorbed. Continue adding stock, about ½ cup at a time, stirring frequently and making sure all the liquid is absorbed before adding more stock. Halfway through cooking the risotto, add the fava beans, reserving a few for garnish. Continue to add stock. Cook until the rice is just tender and creamy but still *al dente*, 15 to 20 minutes. You may have leftover stock.

5 Remove the pan from the heat and stir in the butter, Parmesan cheese, and salt and pepper to taste. Let the risotto rest for a minute or two and serve on individual plates garnished with the reserved fava beans.

Risotto with Green Tomatoes, Crispy Bacon, and Fava Beans.

Risotto with Chicken
Risotto con il Pollo

Leo Schofield, Australia's premier antiques expert, writer, gourmet, food critic, opera buff, and landscaper informs us:

It was a bet between Australia's most celebrated wine personality, Len Evans, and me. Back in the seventies, I discussed with him the possibility of leading a group of food lovers on a tour of Italy. Len said I was wasting my time. There was no market for such an elitist idea. Rising like a trout to fly, I bet him I could get such a trip off the ground and so it was that I discovered the glorious Villa d'Este and its youthful chef and Alain Delon look-alike, Luciano Parolari. My merry band of gourmets and I stayed at the hotel for three days and each day we had cooking lessons. And at one of these lessons, Luciano prepared a sublime chicken risotto.

Now Australia did not lack for Italian food. Massive post-war migration from Europe in the late forties and fifties swelled the country's population and changed its eating habits forever. But the kind of Italian food it brought was southern Italian. Few Aussies had heard of, let alone experienced, a risotto.

On their return home, the amateur and professional chefs who'd comprised my tour group began cooking up a storm. And it was no time before risottos of every stripe began appearing on Melbourne and Sydney's private and public menus. So it can be claimed that this authentic northern Italian dish was launched in Australia by Parolari and the Villa d'Este.

And so we bring to you, the delicious standby that started it all, Risotto with Chicken:

Serves 4 to 6
1 roasted chicken
6 cups chicken stock
4 tablespoons extra virgin olive oil
1 medium onion, finely chopped
2 cloves garlic, chopped
2 cups Carnaroli rice

1 cup dry white wine
2 fresh sage leaves
3 tablespoons butter
⅓ cup grated Parmesan cheese
Salt and freshly ground black pepper to taste
10 sprigs flat-leaf parsley, chopped

1 Remove and clean the bones from the chicken. Dice the meat into small cubes.

2 Combine the bones with the stock in a large saucepan, bring to a boil, then reduce the heat and simmer for 20 minutes. Drain the liquid through a fine sieve. Return to the heat and keep at a bare simmer.

3 Make the risotto by heating 2 tablespoons of the olive oil in a large, heavy saucepan over medium heat. Add the onion and garlic and cook, stirring constantly with a wooden spoon, until softened and translucent, about 3 minutes. Add the rice and cook, stirring, for about 3 minutes, until every grain is coated with oil. Add ½ cup of the wine and stir until absorbed.

4 Add 1 cup of the stock and stir until the liquid is absorbed. Continue adding stock, about ½ cup at a time, stirring frequently and making sure all the liquid is absorbed before adding more stock. Cook until the rice is just tender and creamy but still *al dente*, 15 to 20 minutes. You may have leftover stock.

5 Meanwhile, in a large sauté pan, heat the remaining 2 tablespoons olive oil and lightly brown the chicken. Deglaze the pan with the remaining ½ cup wine, then add the sage. Remove the pan from the heat, cover, and let rest.

6 When the risotto is ready, remove the pan from the heat, and stir in the chicken mixture, followed by the butter, Parmesan cheese, and salt and pepper to taste. Let the risotto rest for a minute or two and serve, topped with the parsley.

Poultry and Meat Risottos

Risotto with Chicken Leftovers
Risotto con Avanzi di Pollo

Sydney-based Bruce Jarrett, like Richard Story, "accidentally" learned the secret behind transforming leftovers into a risotto worthy of praise:

The phone rang just after five p.m. I had forgotten that I was due to play host for a group of friends visiting from New York. I panicked: my favorite butcher and fishmonger would be closed. Now what? I searched the refrigerator. Apart from jam, eggs, and a few things I should have thrown out days ago, I spied some good leftover roast chicken and, fortunately, frozen chicken stock. I raced to the supermarket and bought mushrooms, celery, and berries (for dessert, top these with mascarpone, which can be flavored with brandy or *Amaretto di Saronno* and a little caster sugar). *Risotto con Avanzi di Pollo*, which sounds much better than leftovers, saved the day and was much better than ordering in pizza:

Serves 4 to 6
6 cups chicken stock
1 tablespoon butter
1 tablespoon extra virgin olive oil
1 small onion, finely chopped
2 celery stalks, cut into very small pieces
1 carrot, cut into very small pieces
2 cups Carnaroli rice
½ cup dry white wine (optional)
½ pound mushrooms (any variety), chopped
¾ pound leftover chicken off the bone
Salt and freshly ground black pepper to taste
Chopped parsley or celery leaves, for garnish
2 tablespoons grated Parmesan cheese

1 Bring the stock to a boil in a medium saucepan, then reduce the heat and keep at a bare simmer.

2 Melt the butter with the olive oil in a large, heavy saucepan over medium heat. Add the onion and cook, stirring constantly with a wooden spoon, until softened and translucent, about 3 minutes. Add half the celery and carrots

and sauté for 3 minutes, until softened. Add the rice and cook, stirring, for about 3 minutes, until every grain is coated with butter and oil. Then add the wine, if using, and stir until absorbed.

3 Add 1 cup of the stock and stir until the liquid is absorbed. Continue adding stock, about ½ cup at a time, stirring frequently and making sure all the liquid is absorbed before adding more stock. After 5 minutes of cooking, add the mushrooms, chicken, and remaining celery and carrots. Continue adding stock. Cook until the rice is just tender and creamy but still *al dente*, 15 to 20 minutes. You may have leftover stock.

4 Remove the pan from the heat and add salt and pepper to taste. Let the risotto rest for a minute or two and serve topped with the chopped parsley or celery leaves and the Parmesan cheese on the side.

Risotto with Chicken Livers
Risotto con Fegatini di Pollo

This is the first choice for Jean-Marc Droulers, president and CEO of Villa d'Este. This dish is not popular in America, although it is considered a delicacy both in France and Italy; however, Luciano predicts that it will not be long before risotto-lovers will be clamouring for garnishes such as chicken livers, kidneys, frog's legs, and snails, all of which are on the top of Jean-Marc Droulers' list.

This risotto is easy to make because it follows the same procedure as the *Risotto alla Parmigiana* recipe—all you have to do is prepare the chicken livers separately and add them at the last moment. Perfection!

Serves 6
6 cups chicken stock
4 tablespoons butter
2 tablespoons extra virgin olive oil
1 small onion, finely chopped
2 cups Carnaroli rice
1 cup sparkling wine
6 tablespoons grated Parmesan cheese, plus more for serving
Salt and freshly ground black pepper to taste

Chicken Livers

1 pound chicken livers, trimmed and cut into small pieces
All-purpose flour, for dredging the chicken livers
2 tablespoons butter
Salt and freshly ground black pepper to taste
½ cup Marsala wine
3 sage leaves

1 Bring the stock to a boil in a medium saucepan, then reduce the heat and keep at a bare simmer.

2 Melt 1 tablespoon of the butter with 1 tablespoon of the olive oil in a large, heavy saucepan over medium heat. Add the onion and cook, stirring constantly with a wooden spoon, until softened and translucent, about 3 minutes. Add the rice and cook, stirring, for about 3 minutes, until every grain is coated with butter and oil. Then add ½ cup of the wine and stir until absorbed.

3 Add 1 cup of the stock and stir until the liquid is absorbed. Continue adding stock, about ½ cup at a time, stirring frequently and making sure all the liquid is absorbed before adding more stock. Cook until the rice is just tender and creamy but still *al dente*, 15 to 20 minutes. You may have leftover stock.

4 While the risotto is cooking, prepare the chicken livers: Dredge the chicken livers in the flour. Warm the butter in a large skillet over medium-high heat. When very hot, add the chicken livers and sauté for about 1 minute on each side, until firm and beginning to release their juices. Add salt and pepper to taste. Add the Marsala and cook until absorbed. Add the sage.

5 When the risotto is done, remove the pan from the heat and stir in the remaining 3 tablespoons butter, 1 tablespoon olive oil, the Parmesan cheese, the remaining ½ cup sparkling wine, and salt and pepper to taste. Let the risotto rest for a minute or two and serve on individual plates topped with the chicken livers and additional Parmesan cheese on the side.

Risotto with Herb Infusion and Skewered Chicken and Cherry Tomatoes

Risotto con Infuso di Erbe e Spiedini di Pollo e Pomodorini

Just as we were going to press with this book, the hotel was breaking ground for a kitchen garden where Luciano could daily choose the freshest herbs and vegetables to add to his omelettes, salads, and, of course, his superb risottos. This dish is Luciano's first recipe of many to incorporate the fresh ingredients from Villa d'Este's new kitchen garden.

Serves 6

Herb Infusion (to be used in small quantities to add flavour to risottos, meats, poultry and fish)

1 ounce minced parsley

1 ounce minced basil

½ ounce thyme leaves

¼ ounce minced mint leaves

1 ounce minced rosemary

1 ounce minced lemon rind

½ ounce onion, finely chopped

⅓ ounce minced garlic

¼ cup extra virgin olive oil

Chicken And Cherry Tomato Skewers

¾ pound chicken breast, cut into 1-inch cubes

12 cherry tomatoes

Six 1-inch pieces lemongrass

2 tablespoons extra virgin olive oil

½ cup dry white wine

6 small sprigs of fresh rosemary, chopped

Risotto

6 cups chicken stock

4 tablespoons butter

2 tablespoons extra virgin olive oil

Risotto with Herb Infusion and Skewered
Chicken and Cherry Tomatoes.

1 small onion, finely chopped
2 cups Carnaroli rice
1 cup sparkling white wine
5 tablespoons grated Parmesan cheese
Salt and freshly ground black pepper to taste

1 To make the herb infusion, combine the ingredients in a small saucepan and cook over low heat without boiling for 15 to 20 minutes. Stir and pass through a fine sieve. Reserve.

2 Alternate chicken and cherry tomatoes using the lemongrass as a skewer. Warm the olive oil in a large sauté pan over medium heat. Add the skewers and cook until the chicken is lightly browned on all sides. Add the dry white wine and rosemary and cook until the chicken is tender, about 10 minutes. Set aside on a warmed plate.

3 While you're making the herb infusion and chicken skewers, prepare the risotto: Bring the stock to a boil in a medium saucepan, then reduce the heat and keep at a bare simmer.

4 Melt 1 tablespoon of the butter with 1 tablespoon of the olive oil in a large, heavy saucepan over medium heat. Add the onion and cook, stirring constantly with a wooden spoon, until softened and translucent, about 3 minutes. Add the rice and cook, stirring, for about 3 minutes, until every grain is coated with butter and oil. Then add ½ cup of the sparkling wine and stir until absorbed.

5 Add 1 cup of the stock and stir until the liquid is absorbed. Continue adding stock, about ½ cup at a time, stirring frequently and making sure all the liquid is absorbed before adding more stock. Cook until the rice is just tender and creamy but still *al dente*, 15 to 20 minutes. You may have leftover stock.

6 Remove the pan from the heat and stir in the remaining 3 tablespoons butter, 1 tablespoon olive oil the Parmesan cheese, remaining ½ cup sparkling wine, and salt and pepper to taste. Let the risotto rest for a minute or two and serve on individual plates, topped with chicken skewers and a few drops of the infusion.

Fried Milanese Risotto

Risotto al Salto

In the golden days after a performance at La Scala, it was considered very trendy to meet at the Savini Restaurant in the Galleria of Milan to enjoy a *Risotto al Salto*. It is said that this dish was served in honor of the great Maria Callas. Ever since, this dish has earned a beloved place among opera enthusiasts.

Besides satisfying Callas' distinguished taste, Luciano is always happy to prepare this dish for the critically acclaimed author David Leavitt, who has lived in Italy for many years. After several Villa d'Este experiences, this rice dish became one of the author's favorites.

Serves 6

3 cups leftover Milanese Risotto
  (see recipe page 96) (see Note)
2 tablespoons butter

1 Heat a medium nonstick pan over medium heat and melt 1 tablespoon of the butter. Add the rice and flatten it out over the bottom of the pan with a wooden spoon until it is as thin as a pancake. Sauté until a golden brown crust is formed underneath the rice; lift the rice with a spatula to check.

2 Flip the rice "pancake." (Unlike a breakfast pancake, the rice cannot be flipped so easily. It's best to slip the rice out of the pan onto a plate, top it with another plate, carefully turn the plates upside down, and then slip the rice back into the frying pan.) Before returning the rice to the pan, melt another tablespoon of butter in the skillet. Cook until crisp on the other side. Serve hot.

Note: At Villa d'Este, of course, fried risotto is not made with leftovers but is created anew as a classic Milanese and then fried.

Fried Milanese Risotto.

Green Risotto with Braised Snails

Risotto Verde con le Lumache Brasate

Food has been used as an aphrodisiac for centuries. After trying the Green Risotto with Braised Snails, it's no wonder that good friend Dru Demmy had this to say: "Being given a plate of risotto is a warm, sensuous experience." For a romantic, intimate evening, we recommend this recipe paired, of course, with flutes of champagne.

Serves 6

36 snails
2 tablespoons coarse salt
5 tablespoons butter
1 small carrot, cubed
1 celery stalk, cubed
2 onions, finely chopped
½ clove garlic, chopped
5 cherry tomatoes, peeled and cut into cubes
1½ cups dry white wine
6 cups fish stock
1 tablespoon extra virgin olive oil
2 cups Carnaroli rice
1 ounce cooked green peas, pureed
4 tablespoons grated Parmesan cheese
Salt and freshly ground black pepper to taste

1 Put the snails in a bowl, cover with the coarse salt, and set aside for 6 hours. Place the snails in a colander and wash them under cold running water. Put the snails in a large saucepan, cover with cold water, and bring to a boil, and simmer for about 5 minutes. Drain, then remove the shells and clean the interiors. (It is, or course, easier to buy snails pre-cleaned and precooked.)

2 Warm 1 tablespoon of the butter in a large sauté pan over medium heat. Add the carrots, celery, half of the onion, and the garlic, and sauté for about 5 minutes, until the vegetables have softened. Add the snails and the tomatoes. Pour ½ cup of the wine over the mixture. Cook until the wine is absorbed, then add water to cover .

3 Cook for 1 ½ hours, adding more water if needed.

4 Meanwhile, prepare the risotto: Bring the stock to a boil in a medium saucepan, then reduce the heat and keep at a bare simmer.

5 Melt 1 tablespoon of the butter with the olive oil in a large, heavy saucepan over medium heat. Add the remaining onion and cook, stirring constantly with a wooden spoon, until softened and translucent, about 3 minutes. Add the rice and cook, stirring, for about 3 minutes, until every grain is coated with butter and oil. Then add the remaining 1 cup wine and stir until absorbed.

6 Add 1 cup of the stock and stir until the liquid is absorbed. Continue adding stock, about ½ cup at a time, stirring frequently and making sure all the liquid is absorbed before adding more stock. After about 5 minutes of cooking, add green pea puree. Continue adding stock. Cook until the rice is just tender and creamy but still *al dente*, 15 to 20 minutes. You may have leftover stock.

7 Remove the pan from the heat and stir in the remaining 3 tablespoons butter, the Parmesan cheese, and salt and pepper to taste. Let the risotto rest for a minute or two and serve on individual plates with the snails and their sauce.

Vegetable Soup with Rice
Minestrone con Riso

There are various theories on how to cook minestrone because the process has become a very personal one, with recipes varying from one region to another. Not only do world-renowned chefs have secret recipes, but every Italian does, too. We share our recipe here because it is an Italian staple one simply cannot go without. And it keeps well for several days and can be served either hot or cold, making it an ideal dish year-round.

There are countless variations on this classic: Garlic can be added when sautéing the salt pork and then removed after cooking. A crust of Parmesan cheese will add flavor, and should be removed when the soup is cooked. In the summer, top off the soup with a dollop of pesto for extra flavor (see following recipe). A tablespoon of green Tuscan olive oil can be drizzled on top of each soup bowl when serving. But perhaps the most mouthwatering secret of all is that adding rice will give the minestrone a special risotto-like zest.

Serves 4 to 6
2 to 3 tablespoons extra virgin olive oil
¼ cup diced salt pork (optional)
1 leek, thinly sliced
1 celery stalk, coarsely chopped
2 carrots, coarsely chopped
2 zucchini, coarsely chopped
½ cup trimmed and chopped string beans
2 cups shredded cabbage
2 medium potatoes
2 tomatoes, diced
½ cup green peas
½ cup dried cannelloni beans
1 bay leaf
Salt to taste
1 cup Carnaroli rice, uncooked

1 Warm the olive oil in a 6- to 7-quart pot over medium heat. Add the salt pork, if using, and sauté for 5 minutes. Add the vegetables in the order listed, cooking for 2 to 3 minutes each before adding the next. Add the beans and bay leaf. Cover the vegetables with water, add salt to taste, and cook at a low boil for about 2 hours. About 20 minutes before the soup is finished, add the rice.

Pesto

2 cups fresh basil leaves
1½ cups extra virgin olive oil
¼ cup pine nuts
½ cup grated Parmesan cheese
½ cup grated pecorino cheese
¾ teaspoon chopped garlic

1 While the soup is cooking, make the pesto. The best way to prepare pesto is by hand with a mortar and pestle, but to save time you can make it in a food processor: Put all the ingredients into a food processor and process until smooth.

Pesto freezes well, so save what you don't use for future use.

Rice Balls
Arancini

Sonia Malfi comes from Sicily where, she says, the *arancini*, Italian rice balls made with white wine risotto, are shaped like pears. At Villa d'Este, Luciano serves them with cocktails. No matter how they are served (or shaped), they are delicious!

Serves 4 to 6
1 recipe Milanese Risotto with Saffron (page 96)
⅔ cup mozzarella cheese cut into ¼-inch dice
All-purpose flour, for dredging
1 egg, beaten
¾ cup breadcrumbs
Olive oil, for frying

1 Prepare the basic recipe for Risotto with Saffron. Spread the risotto over a baking sheet and cover with plastic wrap. Set aside to cool or refrigerate overnight.

2 The next day, roll the risotto into walnut-sized balls. Press a hole in the middle of each with your thumb, place some mozzarella cheese inside, and press the risotto around it, shaping it into a ball.

3 Roll each ball first in flour, then beaten egg, followed by the breadcrumbs.

4 Heat the oil to 350°F in a deep-fryer, throw in a piece of bread, and when it turns golden brown, deep-fry the rice balls, in batches, for 3 to 4 minutes each. Remove with a slotted spoon, drain on paper towels, and serve hot.

Rice Balls.

Rice Croquettes
Suppli al Telefono

As if the *arancini* weren't enough, two Roman Villa d'Este employees protested: "How about the *suppli*? Haven't you ever heard of *suppli al telefono*?" But of course! When in Rome it is a treat to stop at Rosati's on *Piazza del Popolo* and together with a *negroni* (the best-known Italian cocktail), eat a couple of *suppli*, which are shaped like croquettes. You don't have to visit Rome in order to eat them, though, because Luciano's recipe can easily be prepared at home and served at your own cocktail party.

The *suppli* are stuffed with more mozzarella cheese than the *arancini*, so when you bite into them the cheese pulls out to resemble strands of telephone wires—hence the name. A little meat sauce can also be added to the center.

The meat sauce is optional, but should be you in an ambitious mood, it's worth making at home. Reserve any leftovers from the *suppli*—either in the freezer or refrigerator—for other meals that need a perfect meat sauce.

Makes 24 croquettes
¾ cup dried porcini mushrooms
2 tablespoons tomato paste
2 cups beef stock
One 16-ounce can Italian peeled plum tomatoes,
   crushed by hand
4 tablespoons butter
2 cups Carnaroli rice
2 eggs
2 cups grated Parmesan cheese
1 onion, chopped
2 ounces prosciutto, finely chopped
7 ounces ground beef
Salt and freshly ground black pepper to taste
5 ounces mozzarella cheese, cut into ¼-inch dice
¾ cup unseasoned breadcrumbs
Olive oil, for frying

1 Soak the mushrooms in 1½ cups of water for 2 hours. Drain the mushrooms, reserving the soaking liquid, and chop finely. Dissolve the tomato paste in the mushroom liquid and set aside.

2 Meanwhile, in a medium saucepan, combine the beef stock, crushed tomatoes, and 3 tablespoons of the butter; mix well and bring to a boil. Add the rice, reduce the heat to a simmer, and cook, stirring occasionally, for 20 minutes. Turn the rice mixture out into a mixing bowl and gradually stir in the eggs and Parmesan cheese. Set aside to cool.

3 Melt the remaining 1 tablespoon butter in a 12- to 14-inch sauté pan over low heat. Raise the heat to high, add the onion and prosciutto, and cook for 3 minutes. Add the ground beef and cook until well browned, about 5 minutes. Add the mushrooms, mushroom-liquid-tomato paste mixture, and salt and pepper to taste, and keep at a simmer.

4 With a spoon, make egg-shaped portions of the rice, and make an indentation in the center of each one. Place 1 teaspoon of filling in the center of each croquette, along with a few cubes of mozzarella cheese. Roll each ball in the breadcrumbs to completely coat, and set aside.

5 Heat the olive oil in a large, heavy-bottomed pot over high heat until almost smoking. In batches, fry the croquettes in the hot oil, turning frequently, until they are golden brown, about 5 minutes. Remove with a slotted spoon and drain on paper towels. Season with salt and pepper to taste. Serve with the meat sauce, if desired.

Rice Croquettes.

Meat Sauce

2 tablespoons butter
2 tablespoons extra virgin olive oil
1 onion, chopped
1 carrot, chopped
½ pound ground beef
½ pound ground veal
½ pound ground pork or sausage
½ cup dried mushrooms, soaked in water and strained
Salt and freshly ground black pepper to taste
1 cup dry red wine
1 tablespoon dried herbs
2 tablespoons tomato paste
One 12-ounce can Italian peeled plum tomatoes, chopped
1 to 2 cups vegetable stock

1 Melt the butter with the olive oil in a large earthenware pot or heavy enameled cast-iron saucepan over medium heat. Add the onion, carrot, and celery and sauté until the onion turns golden, about 5 minutes. Add the ground beef, veal, and pork, the mushrooms, and salt and pepper to taste. Turn the heat up and pour in the wine. When the wine has almost evaporated, lower the heat and add the herbs, tomato paste, and tomatoes. Simmer, stirring occasionally, for about 1 hour (the longer the better), adding a little stock at a time as needed.

Rice Salad
Insalata di Riso

As the only pool of its kind in the world—one that is supported by pontoons over a large body of water—the floating swimming pool on Lake Como is one of Villa d'Este's main attractions. For sunbathers, like visitor Arnold Schwarzenegger and his family, this Rice Salad, or *Insalata di Riso*, is the perfect accompaniment to any relaxing afternoon spent poolside.

Serves 4 to 6

1 tablespoon coarse salt
½ pound long-grain rice (such as Carolina)
2 boiled carrots, diced
2 or 3 boiled zucchini, diced
2 celery stalks, chopped
1 cup diced boiled ham
1 cup diced boiled chicken
1 cup diced Swiss cheese
2 tablespoons chopped flat-leaf parsley
½ cup extra virgin olive oil
Lemon juice to taste
4 hard-boiled eggs, quartered
Salt and freshly ground black pepper to taste

1 Fill a large saucepan with 3 quarts of cold water and the coarse salt. Bring to a boil, then add the rice. Do not cover. Boil the rice, stirring occasionally with a wooden spoon so the grains do not stick to the bottom of the pan, for approximately 15 to 20 minutes, depending on the type of rice, the size of the saucepan, and the heat of the burner.

2 Drain the rice thoroughly into a colander. When the rice is completely dry, transfer to a large bowl and mix in the vegetables, ham, chicken, cheese, and parsley. Add the olive oil and season with lemon juice and salt and pepper to taste.

3 Add the eggs to the salad, or use as a garnish.

Rice-Stuffed Tomatoes

Pomodori Ripieni di Riso

American visitors Ida and Perry Fishbein have been coming to Lake Como for the past thirty-one years. They are convinced that only at Villa d'Este can they enjoy risotto, when it has been cooked by Luciano Parolari.

When eating in the formal Verandah Restaurant, they never bother to order because Chef Luciano develops a new risotto dish to mark the occasion of their visit. Says Perry, "My taste buds come alive and I am already thinking about the next risotto, which is always the best and tops the last one." The following recipe is just one of Luciano's latest and greatest creations.

Serves 4 to 6
6 ripe tomatoes
½ cup uncooked Carnaroli rice
1 tablespoon fresh oregano leaves
1 teaspoon marjoram leaves
1 teaspoon chopped flat-leaf parsley
1 tablespoon chopped basil
¼ cup extra virgin olive oil
Salt and freshly ground black pepper to taste

1 Cut a slice from the top of each tomato to make a cap. Carefully hollow out the tomatoes and strain the flesh into a bowl. Add the rice, herbs, olive oil, and salt and pepper to taste and let stand for about 30 minutes to blend the flavors. Sprinkle the inside of the tomatoes with salt and turn them upside down to drain out their moisture.

2 Preheat the oven to 350°F.

3 Drain the rice and fill the tomatoes with the rice, reserving the tomato liquid.

4 Replace the caps and arrange the stuffed tomatoes in an oiled baking dish. Bake for 2 hours, adding tomato liquid to the pan as needed.

The famous floating pool at Villa d'Este.

The Kitchen Garden at Villa d'Este

Inaugurated in 2003, the kitchen garden at Villa d'Este supplies Luciano Parolari with fresh ingredients for all his recipes, especially for his risottos. It is nestled in the sunny hillside facing Lake Como in the 18-acre botanical garden that surrounds the hotel.

The garden was designed by Emilio Trabella, the landscape architect made famous for his work on the Serre Ratti Cultural Center. Luciano Parolari served as Trabella's muse in the garden design, as it is tailor-made for the chef and his recipes. As Parolari is famous for using of fresh ingredients, especially aromatic spices and herbs, in his dishes, Trabella made this garden an extension of the Villa d'Este kitchen.

Bask in the luxurious view and imagine the scents wafting through the air. . .

perhaps your new risotto creations are deserving of an

inspirational garden, too.

On the hill, on the right side of the Cypress Avenue leading to the Statue of Hercules, is the kitchen garden. It is planted by Luciano and offers a wide selection of fresh herbs, including different types of basil, oregano, parsley, sage and thyme, vegetables, and berries. Every morning Luciano makes his selection of herbs for the dishes of that day and often brings along some of the clients for a tour of the varieties of plants and allowing them to chose what dish they would like to order, based on the fresh herbs they see in the garden.

 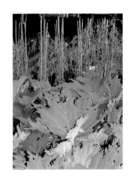

Villa d'Este has been a hotel, now formally known as the Grand Hotel Villa d'Este, since 1873 when a group of ingenious businessmen decided to combine the two buildings on the property—the Queen's Pavilion and the Cardinal's Building—into what is today the hotel. Originally dating back to the fifteenth century when nuns took refuge from the Civil War in 1442, and finally changing hands so that the current Villa main building was built by architect Pellegrino Pelligrini in 1568; it was he who created the landmark landscape as well. At this point the renown of the grounds and buildings of the villa reached far and wide. The year was 1815 when Caroline of Brunswick-Wolfenbuttel, Princess of Wales and future Queen of England made the villa her home (having abandoned her King mere days after their wedding and creating quite a scandal) that the most interesting chapters in the history of the buildings and the gardens began. She renamed the place the New Villa d'Este and since then the villa has become the favorite retreat for well-heeled travelers worldwide… all reveling in the history, architecture, and of course, the finest food northern Italy has to offer: risotto.

Right, Basil in the herb Garden. Above, Buffalo Mozzarella festooned with fresh basil.

With Thanks...

First of all, a big thank you goes to Marta Hallett, publisher of Glitterati, to whom Luciano and I suggested: "How about a book about risottos?" Her immediate reply was, "Great! Let's get going!" And so it all started.

Again (as with past books), the Villa d'Este staff and guests teamed up to put together the recipes. Many frequent Villa d'Este visitors enriched their risotto preferences with anecdotes, which we are sure you will enjoy as much as we did. The friends who helped turn out this book could fill a phone directory and still I might forget some names of those who contributed. Particular thanks go to the following, who urged me to collect Luciano's recipes into this book:

Julie Amsterdam sent many of her clients to Villa d'Este through her wonderful travel agency. Mildred Amico, from the James Beard Foundation, had Luciano prepare a gala dinner in 2002 to celebrate his twenty-fifth anniversary as executive chef of Villa d'Este. The gala started out with Risotto and White Truffle, which has become Mildred's favorite: Many thanks to her, and also to our chef from Villa La Massa, Andrea Quagliarella, who was invited to prepare a gala dinner.

Dr. Jim Bonorris and his wife Lucy Zahran came to Villa d'Este twenty-six years ago on their honeymoon. Since then they have returned at least twice a year, every year. And what risotto does the doctor look forward to savoring: the Champagne Risotto... and when it's in season, it has to be covered with white truffle. From New York, Villa d'Este has welcomed three generations of the Black family. Daniel and Marilyn Black first arrived with their children years ago, and now they bring their grandchildren as well.

When Sara Cooper was working on events planning in Washington, DC, she never had time to cook. Now that she has settled down in San Francisco with husband Chris Barnett, she is waiting for our risotto book to be published so she can learn to duplicate Luciano's recipes. When Jonathan Carson was a little boy, he often accompanied his mother Jane Montant, who was the executive editor of Gourmet magazine. Years later, he arrived with his bride, Diana, on their honeymoon. They have since returned with their offspring, and Jon will continue to think of Villa d'Este as his second home. Of course, he is a fan of chef Luciano and loves all his risottos. And how about the Cahan family from Miami, FL: Linda and Richard, with their daughters Alisa and Halley, have been visiting for about ten years and enjoy having most of their meals in the hotel. Edward de Luca, of the New York gallery D. C. Moore is another devoted risotto fan.

To celebrate the United Nations' fiftieth anniversary, Luciano was invited to assist in preparing the luncheons and the gala dinners that took place throughout the month of April, 1995. In November of that year, Sylvia Howard Fuhrman, Special Representative of the Secretary-General for UNIS, once again invited Luciano, along with Jean-Marc Droulers, President and chief executive officer of Villa d'Este, to the benefit dinner honouring Kofi Annan, at the time Under-Secretary-General for Peace Keeping Operations.

Barbara Fouhy, who worked with one of the top travel agencies in Washington, started a trend that became very popular a few years ago. She collected groups of about fifteen ladies and some gentlemen, all food-lovers, who especially wanted to learn how to make risotto "à la Luciano." They sojourned to both Villa d'Este and Villa La Massa. Some of the participants have returned to Lake Como, like Ron and Sandy Olin, from Asheville, NC, and Rose Marie Hendry and her daughter, Lynne, from San Antonio, TX.

Leda and Jack Frazee from Manhattan, CA, belong to the category of "favorite repeat guests," since they have returned annually, for twelve or more consecutive years. They take practically all their meals in the hotel, so they can enjoy a variety of risottos. Ron and Pat Fidler, who used to live in Como many years ago, still return to Villa d'Este, which they consider their second home. They now live in England, but travel on an annual basis to treat themselves to Luciano's risottos. Fabric designer Alice Gesar Papazian loves the classical *Risotto alla Milanese*. Food editor Camille Glenn of Louisville, KY, opened many doors for Luciano when she invited him nearly thirty years ago to prepare a fund-raising dinner. This was when risotto was introduced for the first time to the elite of Louisville.

Designer Harry Hinson spends his weekends in the country and he always invites some friends to his "risotto parties." His guests, one by one, get to stir the rice for about three minutes; this way, everybody can contribute. The first generation of Kriendlers, founders of the legendary "21 Club," visited Villa d'Este in the late nineteen-forties. The second generation followed, and they were all introduced to Luciano's risottos. Now, we are expecting the third generation to follow. Fred Krehbiel was only a boy when he accompanied his father to Villa d'Este for the first time. A few years have passed since then and he now has a very large family. Every year they return. At the last count, which included some additional business associates, they numbered over fifteen!

Michael Lacher, the *avvocato* (lawyer), as the staff of Villa d'Este would address him, with his wife Judie and son Nicholas, spent many a holiday at Villa d'Este tasting all the risottos. From Sydney, Bernie Leser, one-time president of Conde Nast Publications, is still considered an aficionado of the risotto "king" Luciano. From Palm Beach, youngster Ted Leopold and his brothers started visiting Villa d'Este with their parents. Now Ted travels with his wife Roslyn, and not only do they have all their meals in the hotel, but they never leave the premises!

Beppe Spadacini, the fashion designer born and raised in Cernobbio and now known worldwide, has given Luciano his version of a risotto in which he removes the onion and the mushrooms that typically flavor the rice. Instead, he uses chicken and meat stock, and the best Barolo wine. When TV producer Dawn Smith heard about Spadacini's recipe she commented, "I like that; I have always wanted a Risotto with Barolo." In the late nineteen-seventies a dear friend, Jane Taylor, wife of the former vice -president of TWA, introduced Luciano to the Chevy Chase Club members. To this day, we still keep in contact and many of them visit with us.

From London, Professor Stuart Timperley and his beautiful wife, Veronica, arrive at least twice a year with their daughters… and they definitely like risotto. Veronica favors her risotto with vegetables, and plenty of them. Penny Trenk from New York is always happy to try out a new risotto recipe,

Risotto inspired passion from the artist Lou Brooks.

and she comes with her husband David at least once a year. One of the most faithful families who come year after year to Villa d'Este is Jens and Nina Werner and their sons from Copenhagen.

Yolanda Wright from Fayetteville, NY, is a food editor who loves to spend time in the kitchen watching Luciano stir the risottos. Chiropractor Wayne Winnick came to Villa d'Este for the first time in 1988, and he tries to return whenever possible because he also enjoys Luciano's risottos. Valerie Anne Wilson of the well known Valerie Wilson Travel has a favorite risotto: it should be prepared with a light tomato sauce topped with small zucchini blossoms.

I choose to believe that the magic for the return visitors is an opportunity for each of them to sample some of Luciano's extraordinary and ever-growing repertoire of risottos. And I thank every one of them for their support and enthusiasm in the compilation of this book.

And finally, I must thank my colleague and friend Annamaria Duvia, whose inexhaustible patience made this book possible.

Index